Leadership Development for Educators

Herb Rubenstein,
F. Mike Miles, and Laurie Bassi

D1447392

ROWMAN & LITTLEFIELD EDUCATION

A division of

ROWMAN & LITTLEFIELD PUBLISHERS, INC.
Lanham • New York • Toronto • Plymouth, UK

PUBLISHED BY ROWMAN & LITTLEFIELD EDUCATION

A division of Rowman & Littlefield Publishers, Inc.
A wholly owned subsidary of The Rowman & Littlefield Publishing Group, Inc.
4501 Forbes Boulevard, Suite 200, Lanham, Maryland 20706
http://www.rowmaneducation.com

Estover Road
Plymouth PL6 7PY
United Kingdom

British Library Cataloguing in Publication Information Available

Library of Congress Cataloging-in-Publication Data

Rubenstein, Herb.
   Leadership development for educators/by Herb Rubenstein, F. Mike Miles, and Laurie Bassi.
      p. cm.
   Includes bibliographical references.
   ISBN 978-1-60709-019-9 (cloth : alk. paper) — ISBN 978-1-60709-020-5 (pbk. : alk. paper) — ISBN 978-1-60709-021-2 (electronic)
   1. Educational leadership.   I. Miles, F. Mike, 1956– II. Bassi, Laurie J. (Laurie Jo), 1954– III. Title.
   LB2806.R79 2009
   371.1'06—dc22

                                                                            2009031912

Printed in the United States of America

∞™ The paper used in this publication meets the minimum requirements of American National Standard for Information Sciences—Permanence of Paper for Printed Library Materials, ANSI/NISO Z39.48-1992.

Table of Contents

Acknowledgements

There are more people who have helped shape this book than we could ever acknowledge here. We thank the teachers, librarians, coaches, students, extra-curricular activity supervisors, principals, and school administrators whom we have interviewed and observed over the past year writing this book. We thank those teachers who poured their hearts and their souls into each of us, demanding excellent work, and keeping us motivated in school and in our lives.

We thank our publisher, Rowman & Littlefield, for understanding that the tide is turning now in education, where assisting teachers in becoming better leaders might just be the next "killer app" in education. We also thank the Educational Testing Service and the Educational Commission for the States for taking the position that teacher leadership is important and for devoting its resources to helping this concept become an important innovative step in the evolution of education in America. We thank Teach for America, which includes leadership training for its teachers.

We also thank those to whom we owe the most—our parents. While some of the parents of the three authors never finished high school, others went on to get PhDs. Yet, they all had something in common. They believed in education, and they believed in us. They believed we could learn any subject, and more importantly they believed that we should master the subjects we studied. They often took the side of the teacher in our early development, and they spent time with us on our homework, day in and day out.

Most importantly, we want to acknowledge teachers—the approximately 3,663,000, teachers who are seeking to improve our schools every day, but have not been taught leadership skills. We acknowledge their hard work, their frustration, their high turnover rates, and their challenges in teaching in schools that have limited resources, and we acknowledge their courage for taking on society's most important task, teaching our children and guiding their development.

We acknowledge the parent who had to hire an attorney to get the school bus to pick up her special needs child. We acknowledge the teacher with diabetes who had to fight to get his two periods of nonteaching during the day so he could go home for dialysis. We acknowledge the researchers who have documented that the quality of leadership in schools is a better predictor of student test scores than socioeconomic status. And, finally, we acknowledge the voters who continue to support our schools in these difficult economic times.

Leadership development training for teachers will not solve all of our schools' problems. But, we believe it can play a pivotal role in significantly improving the lives of teachers and PreK–12 education. We accept responsibility for the shortcomings of this book and pledge to continue our work in education as we are confident that our PreK–12 schools will show strong improvement over the next decade.

We acknowledge that teachers are the key to improving our schools. We thank you, our teachers, for giving each of the three co-authors of this book the education we have needed to generate the insights of this book and the commitment to writing this book. We could never have written this book, or much else worthy in life, without your unwavering support.

Preface

Each of the three co-authors has extensive ties to PreK–12 education, with one of us having been a teacher, assistant principal, principal, assistant superintendent, and now the superintendent of a school district. We know that teachers are leaders. Teachers have one unified goal—to help their students learn so they can make the world a better place.

The government estimates there are approximately 3,7663,000 PreK–12 teachers in the United States, and the authors estimate there are in excess of 2,000,000 classrooms in the United States for PreK–12 students. Our schools are not only one of the most important parts of society they are instrumental to our nation's continued success in this new age of global competition.

A fundamental premise of this book is that as teachers develop their leadership skills, schools will improve. To assist teachers to become better leaders, this book calls for more leadership training for teachers. This book is one small effort to promote and provide leadership training for every PreK–12 school teacher in the United States.

Leadership development is a hot topic in education. Over the past decade substantial resources have been spent to provide leadership training for principals, assistant principals, and school board members, and since 1998, in order to receive a master's in library science, a person must take leadership courses. This book extends the call for this leadership training to include all teachers in PreK–12 education.

The leadership development exercises for teachers in this book are designed to be fun, just as they are designed to be instructive and rewarding. We expect and hope that many books, seminars, and programs for leadership development for teachers will follow this book. We have included a research agenda as an appendix to guide education policy makers regarding how best to build a solid knowledge base on leadership development for teachers.

It is our hope that this book is useful to those who are studying to be teachers, those who are teachers, and those who have been teachers and have retired. Retired teachers and school administrators can play a very important role in promoting leadership development among teachers by studying leadership development themselves and working with teachers who seek to become better leaders.

Leadership development for educators, specifically PreK–12 teachers, is one of a number of approaches that can help PreK–12 education improve our schools and improve the reputation of our schools. Improving our schools and our schools' reputation will encourage our society to devote more resources to this most important endeavor.

Becoming a better leader starts with a commitment to become a better leader and action now to begin to realize and stay true to that commitment. Every teacher has the potential of becoming a better leader. We hope this book is a useful tool and an important step for teachers in the journey to become better leaders.

Herb Rubenstein
Mike Miles
Laurie Bassi
May, 2009
Denver, Colorado Springs, and Golden, Colorado

Introduction

Are Teachers Leaders?

LEADERSHIP AT ALL LEVELS

Educational professionals are under intense pressure to reform the public schools. The need to keep pace with a flatter world and to prepare our students for a fundamentally different workplace add to our teachers' longstanding challenges, such as low graduation rates, large achievement gaps, and the steady decline of performance relative to other industrialized nations. For their part, schools and districts have tried numerous programs and initiatives to improve student achievement. Much discussion centers around the level of resources needed to reform schools or the lack of investment in our education system overall.

While debates about how best to improve schools and how much to invest in public education will undoubtedly continue, there is little doubt that significant changes are needed and that an increasingly global environment intensifies the search for solutions. It is also clear that the pace of change and the transformative nature of proposed reforms will require strong leadership *at all levels.*

If school systems are to be successful in transforming, they will need effective leadership at both the administrative level and among teachers and other employees. Effective superintendents and leaders of any large organization have always known that leadership cannot be equated to a title and that leadership density is what enables the organization to sustain good performance. Yet, in education, not enough has been invested in the research and development of teacher leadership. Strong research suggests that principal leadership makes a difference in how well a school performs (see, for example, McRel). There is less research available on teacher leadership.

Still, anyone who has ever worked in a school can describe how teachers have led. Teachers lead committees, chair departments, organize and manage projects, design curricula, initiate activities, collaborate with colleagues, interact directly with parents and the community, and make numerous decisions daily that affect the welfare of students. Many teachers help develop other teachers and inspire others to do their best work. Indeed, we believe that everyone has leadership potential and can grow as leaders.

That the education profession has done too little to tap this leadership potential is partly evidenced by the fact that many teachers do not identify themselves as leaders. Recognizing that one has enormous leadership potential and that one's leadership capacity can be developed may be the most important step in the growth of a leader. Furthermore, the same recognition—that everyone has leadership potential that can be developed—may be the most important step in an organization's journey from good to great.

WHAT GOOD TEACHER LEADERSHIP LOOKS LIKE

Schools that want to improve classroom instruction first spend time and energy describing what good instruction looks like. A good school trying to become a great school will most likely have a rubric that describes in fair detail what distinguished teaching looks like. Moreover, the rubric is likely to outline observable behaviors and include measurable actions. Rubrics abound in the education profession because school leaders know that if you cannot describe the outcome, it is very difficult to attain it.

Similarly, if a school or district is to build leadership capacity, it must attempt to define what good leadership looks like. Unfortunately, most schools make no attempt to describe leadership behaviors for teachers. Except in this book, one will be hard pressed to find a leadership rubric for teachers and other staff members.

School administrators fail to describe leadership expectations and goals for teachers partly because they usually do not believe that teachers are also leaders. A larger perception problem may also account for the failure to develop teacher leadership: administrators and other titled leaders associate leadership with discrete events and positions rather than the skills and talents of an individual.

Take, for example, how principals generally groom teacher leaders: they tap them to chair a new committee, invite them to participate in a budget meeting, task them with a special project, and generally give them greater responsibilities. To be sure, these sorts of opportunities are important and can help build the capacity of certain individuals, but it is much too limited in scope, failing to take into account the leadership capacity of the rest of the staff and a concept of leadership that is not directly tied to a position or a project.

This book contends that a good leader remains a good leader regardless of the position she has or the length of the project she directs. One can also demonstrate excellent leadership skills in a "follower" role. This is so because leadership is something you carry with you—inside you. It is not something that can be bestowed.

WHO SHOULD READ THIS BOOK

If schools and districts are to become more effective and also sustain reform, they must begin to expand leadership capacity at all levels. This book can help. It provides a framework of leadership that outlines leadership skills and abilities for teachers and provides a guide for organizations that seek to develop the leadership capacity of the staff.

This book is not about helping a teacher climb the administrative ladder to principal or superintendent (although one of our authors has done just that). This book is about giving teachers a good review of sound leadership theory and practices, a clear explanation of how to apply this leadership theory and practices in the classroom and in their lives, and activities that teachers can do alone or in group settings with other teachers to improve their leadership skills.

Teachers can use this book to develop leadership skills that will make them more effective in or out of the classroom. More important—organizations will find this book useful because it can be a catalyst to creating a new appreciation of the value of leadership at all levels and its potential for improving student outcomes, teacher satisfaction, and longevity in the profession; improving the quality of schools overall; and improving public support for the bedrock institution in our society—PreK–12 education.

HOW THIS BOOK IS ORGANIZED

This book begins with an overview of why we believe teachers are leaders and why we believe that improving the leadership capabilities of teachers nationwide will have a significant positive impact on our schools, our teachers, and our PreK–12 students. Chapter Two presents a leadership rubric, the four levels of leadership, to help teachers fully grasp how they can improve their leadership abilities in the process of working in our schools.

Chapter Two includes specific leadership exercises that will help teachers be successful in leadership development. This chapter also includes stories from PreK–12 schools where we are able to demonstrate effective and less-than-effective leadership efforts. Chapter Three provides key insights into how teachers can expand their leadership capacity at each of the four levels of leadership identified in Chapter Two.

Chapter Four discusses leadership focusing on key subgroups in the PreK–12 educational setting. These groups are librarians, coaches, special needs teachers, supervisors of extracurricular activities, and students. Each group has unique leadership needs, training, and abilities, and it is the goal of this chapter to use leadership development as a tool that could help integrate these groups and improve the relationships among these groups in our schools.

Chapter Five presents ten leadership theories and ten leadership principles, discusses motivation, and provides important checklists of well-known, successful leadership approaches. This chapter is a chapter that teachers may wish to refer back to time and again as they pursue their path toward becoming better leaders.

Chapter Six tackles the big question of how improved leadership development among teachers could contribute to systemic change in schools. This chapter states clearly that improving leadership development among teachers is not a silver bullet that will transform schools overnight. This chapter does point out some positive and hopeful ways that schools, students, the teaching profession, and the community will all react positively to improved leadership capabilities by teachers.

Chapter Seven returns us back to the practical side of improving leadership development by teachers. This chapter includes ten steps and exercises that teachers can start undertaking now to improve their leadership.

After the conclusion of the book, there are three very important Appendices. Appendix A includes additional leadership development exercises for teachers. This appendix also describes an approach where teachers can form groups to help each other become better leaders. In this section we discuss 62 topics that teachers can discuss in their leadership groups that will contribute to teachers becoming better leaders.

In Appendix B of the book, we outline approximately 90 "brands" or styles of leadership currently identified in the literature on leadership. After reading this important appendix, teachers will be able to identify more readily their own leadership style and the leadership styles of others. Finally, in Appendix C, we outline our thoughts and recommendations for a future research agenda to support leadership development for teachers.

This book serves as a guide to teachers, the teaching profession, and educators at all levels on how and why to undertake the task of improving leadership skills and abilities for teachers throughout our nation. This book builds on a literature that has been developing over the past thirty years and may now be coming into its own. We believe the demand for leadership development courses and professional credit for teachers who take these courses will increase substantially in the very near future. Librarians have been taking leadership courses to obtain their professional certificates now for over a decade.

Teachers lead every day. This book is designed to support teachers in becoming better leaders, and it is designed to assist school administrators and educational funding agencies appreciate the true potential that improving leadership abilities by teachers can contribute successfully to improving our PreK–12 schools in the United States.

Chapter 1

Why Leadership Development for Teachers and Why Now?

Now is the time to expand the promise of education.

—President Barack Obama, February, 2009

THE CHALLENGES EDUCATORS FACE TODAY

Teachers in the United States in the PreK–12 system know better than anyone the challenges they face every day. Many teachers have to dip into their own pockets to buy supplies for their classrooms. Many teachers are frustrated with those who make the big decisions in their schools. Behavioral problems and challenges from students take up precious teaching time from almost every teacher. School enrollments have fluctuated so much over the past decade that class sizes have mushroomed.

School bond issues have been voted down, placing the entire future of our public school systems in jeopardy. Teachers are tired. Many quit teaching after just a few years. Some schools cannot find enough qualified teachers. Teacher salaries are low. School dropout rates are high, and student achievement in many locales is low. Across the board, student achievement is not increasing to keep up with the new educational demands of our economy. Parents are frustrated.

School superintendents are being fired at an alarming rate. Recent federal mandates developed without significant input from teachers themselves added additional burdens on schools but did not give them the resources necessary to deal with these new burdens. Today, no one denies there are serious challenges in our PreK–12 schools, be they public, chartered, private, or home schooled environments.

THE POTENTIAL FOR IMPROVED
LEADERSHIP SKILLS OF TEACHERS

Improved leadership skills by teachers will not overnight address each and every one of these concerns. But, improved leadership skills by teachers will help our teachers, our school systems, and all stakeholders in our PreK–12 educational process be better equipped to address these issues. We find no challenge in education today, as big as each one is and as long as the list can be made, to be insurmountable.

Teachers with great leadership skills can make great strides in improving the culture of their schools, getting the resources they seek to educate our youth, and finding greater satisfaction in their work. Teachers who are good leaders can promote improved student achievement and help us find better ways to measure student achievement than the types of standardized tests being used today.

Teachers can become better spokespersons for schools and participants in our nation's renewed effort to find the right funding systems that guarantee schools proper funding and teachers proper salaries. This book will present key leadership strategies to deal with these and many other challenges faced by the world of PreK–12 education in general, and teachers in particular.

There are hundreds of definitions of leadership in the literature on this vast subject. There are nearly 100 documented "styles" of leadership and they are listed in Appendix B. No one definition, like no one style, of leadership is perfect for every occasion. But we offer teachers a definition of leadership that is results-oriented and helps us identify when we are acting as leaders and when we are not. That definition is:

Leadership is the creation and fulfillment of worthwhile opportunities by honorable means.

A key element of leadership is the ability to see or identify an opportunity. Leaders often identify and acknowledge problems before others. But, they know their role is never merely to identify a problem or merely complain about it or dwell on it. A leader's role also includes communicating the problem to others so that they can assist in helping solve the problem. Plus, a job of a leader is to work diligently toward identifying potential solutions, and organizing people and resources to help bring about a solution, or at least a significant improvement, in the situation.

Many teachers identify a problem in their schools well before principals or administrators identify the problem. One first year teacher in the Bronx this past year was not told whether he would be teaching physics or chemistry or how many classes of one or the other until less than one week before school started. What a challenging way to start off your career in teaching. Although no single leadership skill or attribute might be able to help this teacher solve the problem he faced, he could use his leadership skills to help make changes so this did not happen to him or any other teacher the following year.

LESSONS OF LEADERSHIP

This example of the teacher in the Bronx yields several important leadership lessons. Leaders often cannot solve problems immediately. Leaders can communicate the problem immediately and have a duty to do so. Leaders must see what is possible to solve the problem. Leaders must take problems and create worthwhile opportunities out of the problems. Silence in the face of a problem is not an option for a leader. Knowing to whom to communicate a problem and how to communicate it so that it starts a process toward dealing effectively with the problem is a challenge that leaders face every day. Good leadership gets this process going quickly.

People who are not skilled in leadership often do not communicate the problem in a manner that starts an effective process toward resolving the problem. This book will guide teachers on how to make this first step in problem identification and problem communication be an effective one. Leaders learn over time how to communicate effectively to stimulate dialogue and to secure resources necessary to resolve problems. It is both an art and a skill.

Sometimes we say the right thing to the wrong person and we stir up challenges, lost time and effort, and increased frustration that could have been avoided if the leader had a more effective communication plan about the problem or challenge. In this book we devote time to helping teachers become more effective communicators when raising problems and issues in the school setting.

A second important lesson of leadership especially valuable to teachers is that leadership is not simply an act that one does once or twice. Leadership is a way of handling challenges and fulfilling opportunities. You will be challenged as a leader. You can only fight so many fights at one time, and you will have to choose which fights to fight, which challenges represent the highest priority to you, and which opportunities you will pursue with all of your vigor.

LEADERS AND STAKEHOLDER: A KEY RELATIONSHIP

When leaders communicate a problem, with the intention of helping lead others to become part of the solution, leaders communicate to stakeholders. A stakeholder is a person, or institution, that has a strong interest in a problem and who will benefit if a good solution is identified and implemented. We recommend broadly defining the stakeholder group when communicating about a problem so as to include all of the people and resources that can be brought together to help address a problem or challenge.

Thus leaders perform a "stakeholder identification process" to establish how best to identify those with whom the leader should communicate about the problem and those with whom to work to help resolve the problem or implement new strategies to improve situations and outcomes in schools. Stakeholders can serve as effective co-leaders in both defining the problem, in proposing a solution, in obtaining needed resources, and in implementing a solution.

Leadership, sustainable leadership, as we define it, is about achieving successful results by honorable means. Teachers, acting as leaders, when seeking to realize an improvement or opportunity in the school setting, should seek to engage all key stakeholders in this effort. Teachers should learn how to include students, parents, administrators, other teachers, union representatives, staff, plus community leaders in the area. in their effort to achieve a worthwhile school goal, fix a school related problem, or fulfill a potential opportunity identified by the teacher.

Leaders must recognize that some will not participate, follow, or act as a co-leader with the teacher in pursing the goal of fixing a problem or improving the school. Some will oppose everything that represents change, even if it is clearly change for the better. Leaders know their opposition and know their opposition's arguments and political power. Leaders must be prepared to face stiff resistance.

LEADERSHIP, ENTHUSIASM, AND STAMINA

Being a leader does not mean you win every fight or are effective in resolving every problem. It does mean that you never let yourself grow too tired, too disillusioned, too apathetic, too disgruntled, to continue to work hard to create an opportunity that will benefit students and teachers in your school and in your school district. Improving your leadership skills will improve your level of enthusiasm and will help you create the attitude and approaches that help promote your stamina in dealing with the many challenges school face.

Improving leadership skills is just like improving your skills at hammering nails in wood. The better you get at it, the more nails you can hammer, and the less effort you have to expend doing it. When a teacher becomes a better leader, that teacher will be better able to secure more resources, including more money, people, and interest, in resolving a problem or dealing effectively with a challenge. When a teacher becomes a better leader the more value the teacher can create for the school, for the student, and for the teacher. Creating more value by a leader inspires a leader to tackle bigger and bigger challenges and become an even better leader.

TEACHERS LEADING STUDENTS AND THEIR SCHOOLS

In addition to teaching students, teachers have always been leaders of students. Teachers, acting as leaders, can become more effective in promoting President Obama's call for now being the time for students to be taught and realize that grades and graduation do matter. The higher the unemployment levels in this country, the more an employer will use grades and graduation as legitimate screening devices when hiring people under twenty years of age. The days when every student could get a job regardless of what they learned in school and what grades they made are over, maybe for a full decade.

With colleges and community colleges seeing their budgets tighten, colleges and community colleges may not be able to accept all students and will need to select students, in part, based on grades and their ability to do well in college courses. Teachers, acting as leaders, are in the best position in society, other than parents, to deliver this message to students in an effective and cogent manner.

In essence, teachers acting as leaders can become more effective in helping students from all walks of life to realize that doing well in school is now more important than ever in living a good life in America. It is leadership that awakens insight in others and informs others effectively of truths and especially new truths in our society. Leaders gain the respect of others. As teachers become better leaders, students will listen more carefully to their words and heed their advice. Leaders deliver the message clearly and the message is: Do poorly in school and your chances of having a good job and earning a good living are not good.

Budgets and money coming from the school districts and public funds are getting tighter with the recession of 2008–2010. Schools need, with teachers serving as co-leaders in this effort, to reach out to the business community, foundations, parents, and all possible resource sources, to capture the financial, in-kind, and other resources our schools need to serve students well.

Even with this tough economy, many employers and many foundations are making huge investments in PreK–12 education.

The Annenberg and Gates Foundations and companies such as Motorola, with its $5 million dollar after school programs to teach science, technology, engineering, and math (STEM), represent just the tip of the iceberg of non-governmental organizations that are willing to put money into our educational system even in these challenging economic times. As teachers become better leaders they can become better advocates for schools and become more successful in helping schools obtain additional funding from nongovernmental organizations.

IMPROVING LEADERSHIP WILL IMPROVE TEACHER EFFECTIVENESS

Improved leadership development, we believe, can be instrumental in helping teachers to become better teachers. Larger and larger class sizes require exponentially greater leadership skills by teachers to reach and connect with every student. Delivering the subject matter to diverse student populations requires greater leadership skills than delivering the subject matter to students from the same backgrounds as the teachers and fellow students.

The efforts toward "mass customization" of education, the integrating of special educational students into classes with other students, the inclusion of gifted students whose home life provides awesome educational opportunities through the Web, tutors, role models, and the like, all require a new set of leadership skills not required when these populations were isolated in schools.

All of these large social issues impact education in a way that demands that teachers have improved leadership skills to navigate the rugged landscape that education presents today. We have thousands of school districts and hundreds of thousands of schools in the United States. Now with the internet, teachers from one school district can mentor and work with teachers from other school districts to become better leaders. School districts should encourage this. Teachers who want to become better leaders can now reach across district lines, even state and regional lines, to become better leaders and to help other teachers become better leaders.

Teachers do not need anything from school districts to become better leaders. Teachers can take on this responsibility to become better leaders all by themselves. We encourage school districts to pay for leadership development programs for teachers and to give teachers real incentives to become better leaders. We encourage teachers' unions to help develop and pay for leadership development programs that will assist teachers in becoming better leaders. But, ultimately, it is up to each teacher, either alone or in groups, to recognize that becoming a better leader will have great benefits for the teacher, and to make a strong commitment to be a better leader.

LEADERSHIP AND IMPROVING EDUCATIONAL OUTCOMES

Every teacher wants to see improved educational outcomes. The leadership development ideas, theories, strategies, practices and approaches in this book are one set of strategies that can play a part in improving educational outcomes. They are also a start to improve teacher and faculty morale, and teacher engagement. Improved leadership abilities by teachers can improve student outcomes. We predict that improving the leadership abilities of all teachers will reduce the number of teachers who leave the profession.

We also believe that improving the leadership abilities of teachers will have a trickle up effect of improving the leadership abilities of principals and administrators, and improve the relationships between teachers and principals. Improving the leadership abilities of teachers can significantly reduce the incidence of students dropping out, reduce student cheating, and we predict, will have a positive impact on student behavioral problems. Ultimately, improving the leadership abilities of teachers across the board will lead to improving educational outcomes.

Leadership development is not the "silver bullet." But improving the leadership capabilities of teachers is one area often neglected by our educational system. There have been vast improvements made in the general area leadership development used by businesses and nonprofit organizations area over the past 40 years. These improvements in how we teach leadership and how people can teach themselves and each other leadership skills can now make a significant difference in our educational environment.

While we cannot make any promises that becoming a better leader will improve your quality of life as a teacher, or improve the educational outcomes of any single student, we think the evidence is clear that the leadership development industry has become a multibillion dollar industry because improving the leadership abilities of people improves their ability to create value in society. We know of no group, no profession, more than the profession of teacher, PreK–12 teacher, that currently creates more value for society in America. Leadership development and teacher development should go hand-in-glove in the future.

FITTING IN BECOMING A BETTER LEADER IN A TEACHER'S ALREADY BUSY SCHEDULE

It is our goal that PreK–12 teachers and the entire educational system in the United States will come to accept that idea that teachers have a duty to be excellent leaders. This duty has been accepted already in many areas of society as employees and managers in industry and the commercial sector now, more than ever, realize that they have a duty to be excellent leaders.

We know duty represents a big commitment. However, the school environments, including the home schooled environment, in America are special places, occupied by special people—teachers. The last thing we want to do is add yet another duty to our teachers' already overworked days. Yet, as teachers develop a stronger and stronger identity as a leader, and as teachers develop better and better skills as a leader, teachers will become even better at time management and delegation of tasks. As teaches accept the duty to becoming better leaders, we think that opportunities will grow in number for teachers and burdens will decline.

Improving one's leadership abilities brings with it many gifts. The ability to work better and more effectively with others, including superiors and those viewed as subordinates. It affords one the ability to gather more resources with greater and greater ease. It provides additional energy and enthusiasm to help one get through the day. It helps one create both long term and short term meaningful visions of how things can be done better. It promotes focusing on results than the challenges of getting to the desired result.

CONCLUSION

Leadership can bring a renewed and rejuvenated perspective to the daily life of a teacher. Every day a teacher can spark in a student a new sense of love of learning and the joy of discovery. Every day a teacher can promote confidence in a student and can lead that student to want to learn more about a subject. Every day a teacher can help a student achieve a good grade and have more pride. Every day a teacher can improve the life of a student. It takes well developed leadership skills to be effective in these activities and all teachers can become better leaders.

Chapter Two provides teachers important insights into four levels of leadership for teachers. It is written to apply directly to the teacher's role in education. It gives teachers a short overview of leadership approaches that are directly relevant to teachers. It also includes some basic leadership practices that all teachers can begin using right away to begin to train and develop leadership skills that will be useful in the classroom, in the entire school building, and in the daily lives of teaches outside of the school building.

Chapter 2

Improving Leadership through Understanding the Four Levels of Leadership

A LEADERSHIP FRAMEWORK THAT APPLIES TO TEACHERS

Stories about teachers using their leadership skills can be found every day in every school. In addition, stories about teachers not using good leadership skills can also be found every day in every school. One theme that we will come back to again in this chapter is the story of two teachers in the same schools who walk into adjacent rooms. They enjoy teaching, have positive attitudes, and are raising student academic proficiency. One is a well-trained and capable leader; the other has not yet received any significant leadership training.

What makes a teacher a leader? What helps turn a teacher into a leader? What distinguishes a strong leader who can set goals and work either alone or with successful teams to achieve them? What is it about some people who are able to get the best out of themselves and others on a regular basis? Why do some people refuse to take on leadership responsibilities or fail when they accept these leadership responsibilities? This chapter will answer these important questions in ways that teachers can use right away to become better leaders.

WHAT LEADERSHIP LOOKS LIKE

In order for teachers to become better leaders, teachers must gain a clearer picture of "what leadership looks like." This chapter paints that picture and assists teachers improve their leadership ability. We have found that having a framework or rubric for understanding leadership development is a critical underpinning to improving as a leader. This chapter provides such a leadership framework. This chapter is designed to operate both on the individual level and the organizational level. At the individual level it is our goal to help teachers become better leaders in their classrooms, in their schools and in their lives.

As we stated before, when leaders lead best, they help others become better leaders. We say they increase the leadership culture or the leadership density around them. By assisting individual teachers become better leaders, by assisting teachers who are good leaders to help other teachers just gaining leadership skills and abilities become better leaders, you can expand the leadership density of your educational institution. Just reading and studying a book, a framework, and leadership rubrics, can only be a start in that direction.

Improved leadership capability, what we call leadership development, requires action learning, real leadership behavior tried in the real world where there are real consequences and real stakes. The exercises we provide throughout this book will assist you in being a better leader in your educational organizational environments and elsewhere throughout your life.

Those who lead great organizations, and even followers in those organizations, understand that leadership at all levels makes a difference. Leadership at every level is a phrase more in use today than ever before. *Leadership density* is a phrase that captures the combined leadership capabilities of those working together in an organization for the organization and its stakeholders' good.

As more and more research allows us to calculate more accurately the leadership capabilities and the willingness of teachers to act as leaders in schools, we expect that the research will show that:

- the higher the leadership capabilities of the teachers in a school,
- the higher the willingness of teachers to act as leaders in schools,
- the higher the educational performance of students will be in the school,
- all other things being equal

In Appendix C we provide a research agenda that can make great headway in testing this hypothesis. What we know now from empirical studies discussed in this book is that the leadership capabilities of principals have a significant impact on students' performance. We believe an even stronger impact will be achieved on student performance by improved leadership capabilities of teachers.

THREE POSTULATES

This chapter outlines a framework for understanding leadership and developing leadership capacity. The leadership framework is based on three postulates:

1) Leadership Skills can be Learned and Developed

The age-old debate of whether truly great leaders are born or made is answered by the experience of the three authors of this book. Each author has studied leadership theory and practice. Each has been and is an educator. Each has become a better leader through study and training and through applying that study and leadership training day in and day out in the real world.

Years of experience in leadership development leaves us with no doubt that much of leadership can be taught. While not everyone will be or wants to be a leader, everyone has leadership potential. Everyone has some capacity to lead. Great organizations invest millions of dollars each year in leadership development precisely because leadership capacity can be developed and leadership potential can be tapped.

2) Leaders Act When it is Appropriate to Act

It is not enough to understand leadership theory, definitions, styles, or rubrics. It is useful to be a student of leadership theory to be a great leader, but it is not sufficient. Leaders act. It is important for leaders to say the right things and to communicate well. But more important than what they say—is what they do. At the end of the day, it is the behaviors and approaches that show how good leadership is performed. It is always behaviors more than the words that inspire and generate the additional, coordinated actions of others that are necessary to produce the desired results.

In addition to behaviors, leaders know attitude makes a huge difference. Hope is more than an attitude. Fear is more than an attitude. But, they are, in part, based on attitudes. Leaders know they are responsible for developing and maintaining the appropriate attitude in each circumstance where they lead. Attitude affects not only how we act but our potential for action. Leaders always strive to reach their potential and help others reach their potential.

We know that leadership capacity can be measured and one can provide objective feedback to persons regarding their leadership capabilities. The framework that we have developed is especially geared to teachers since it is based on our understanding of how every day teachers lead students, parents, other teaches, and school officials at every level.

As we will show, some days some teachers are performing primarily at level one leadership, others, level two, three, or four. By creating these four levels of leadership, we have created a context that teachers can use to understand their current behavior and the current behavior of those they observe, as well as develop new behavioral patterns and approaches that will help them to move closer to acting more consistently as level three or four leaders.

3) Leadership Density is Essential to Improve Schools

According to Thomas Sergiovanni, and many others, one strong leader cannot make an organization great without the support and leadership of others in that organization. This is as true for teachers as it is for administrators in a school setting. It is the leadership density—the combined leadership capacity of all teachers (and individuals at all levels of the organization) that enables a school to achieve its potential, that enables teachers and administrators to achieve their potential, and most importantly, allows and promotes students learning and performing at their highest potential.

More recently, Michael Fullan, author of ***Leadership and Sustainability***, wrote that "there is no chance that large-scale reform will happen, let alone stick, unless capacity building is a central component of the strategy for improvement." We agree. Assisting teachers to want to become better leaders and assisting teachers in becoming better leaders is the contribution this book and its authors seek to make in improving "capacity building" among teachers.

For years, it has been acknowledged and promoted that it is important for principals and administrators be effective leaders. This book stakes out a new claim. That claim is that it is equally, if not more important, for teachers to be effective leaders. From the worlds of business, athletics, government, and the nonprofit sectors, every great organization has learned that to become excellent and to remain excellent by improvement and innovation, people at all levels of the organization must be effective leaders.

In the school district where one of our authors serves as superintendent, the district conducts leadership academies for teachers and support staff alike. So committed is this school district to the notion of leadership density that there is a Community Leadership Academy for parents and other stakeholders. Thus, our leadership model is designed to assist leaders at all levels, especially teachers.

ONE TEACHER'S UNSUCCESSFUL EFFORTS AT LEADERSHIP

The story below sheds great light on leadership and its value to schools. The quality of the instruction of the teachers in the math department of North Lake Junior High was generally poor and student achievement results were low and flat. Sally stood out as one of the exceptions; she was a great classroom teacher of 7th graders. Because of her content knowledge and competency with curriculum alignment and instructional strategies, she was selected as the math department chair. So, by virtue of her position, Sally became one of the school's "teacher leaders."

Playing to her strengths, Sally worked hard and continued to research strategies that would help her and her colleagues teach more effectively. She regularly met with teachers in her department to discuss student achievement data and activities for teaching math. She drafted model unit plans and gave them to her colleagues, encouraging them to follow the plans. In many ways, it looked like Sally was being a good leader.

Despite Sally's efforts, the math department continued to struggle. A couple of the teachers began to emulate her instructional technique with success, since they were superior teaching materials and methods to the ones the teachers had used in the past. However, most of the teachers in the department refused to adopt the new instructional techniques and adopt her superior teaching methods. In fact, they did not change anything they did. They just continued their past practices, which were producing poor results by everyone's measure.

One math teacher was particularly resistant to Sally's suggestions, not only refusing to change her ways but also exerting significant effort to influence other teachers to ignore Sally's model unit plans. Overall, this teacher seemed to have even greater influence over the teaching behavior of the rest of the department than Sally because most of the teachers in the department never changed their behavior in response to Sally's leadership or lack of leadership.

Over time, Sally became frustrated and held fewer department-wide meetings. She focused on the two or three teachers who seemed to be receptive to her suggestions and began to ignore the other teachers. The department continued to struggle and one could argue that Sally abdicated her leadership role. Finally, Sally came into her principal's office and requested that someone else take over the duties of department chair. "These teachers are intractable," she said. "I've always been able to lead by example, but they won't follow my lead. Maybe I'm not the right person for the job."

Sally was, in some respects, a leader. She had great leadership potential. But, she was not able to generate the support from other school teachers and school leaders to demand and secure all math department teachers to begin using the superior materials she had developed. She needed other school leaders to help her move beyond her "level one" leadership capabilities. Level one leadership, which will be explained below, is the ability to assess yourself and assess a current situation.

Sally knew her strengths and weaknesses. She knew what the problem was, poor instructional techniques. She relied on her strengths to create improved instructional techniques, but that is as far as her leadership capability could take her and the math department. She was capable at level one, self-assessment and problem assessment, but not a capable level two leader. A level two leader is also able to understand the environment in which he or she leads, and understand those whom she tries to lead.

A leader competent at level two uses this understanding of the situation and those whom she is trying to lead to help achieve success in reaching the goal that requires all parties working together to reach that goal. It is this understanding of those whom you are trying to lead and the overall situation in which you are trying to lead that is critical to being successful in leading others to act in a manner that improves the situation, solves the problem, or achieves the goal.

The remainder of this chapter will guide the reader through the four levels of leadership. These levels of leadership are the building blocks teachers can begin using today to become better leaders themselves and to help other teachers become better leaders. In general, leaders who can only operate at level one are just starting to think about themselves as leaders.

Level one leaders are those who are beginning to assess his or her strengths and weaknesses as a leader. It must be said that in some areas of life a person can be a level one leader, while in others areas of their lives they can rise to the level of a level four leaders. As we explain the four levels of leadership, look in your own life to see at what level of leadership you operate in the classroom, in the overall school setting, and in important areas of your live.

What is important to know is that even level one leaders are people trying to be leaders.

It is a great step to become a level one leader from a previous position of not being willing to be a leader at all. It represents growth in exactly the right direction of becoming a better leader. And level one is the right place to start for everyone who does not consider themselves a leader, but is willing and eager to become a better leader.

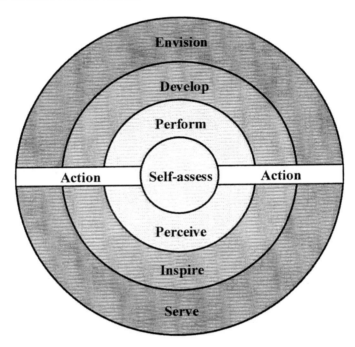

FOUR LEVELS OF LEADERSHIP

Level One Leadership

In Shakespeare's *Hamlet*, Polonius advises his son: "To thine own self be true, and it must follow as the night the day—thou canst not then be false to any man." This is the first axiom for any leader, and it sits at the core of the educator's leadership framework. Before one can lead others, the person must know who he or she is. Each person to be a leader must engage in a rigorous act, we call self-assessment.

Self-Assessment

The first level of leadership is described and fueled by self-awareness. Good leaders understand their talents, preferences and what they think of themselves is consistent with what others think of them. This is congruence. They understand their personality traits and leadership style or styles. They also understand their strengths and weaknesses. They act to take advantage of their strong points and mitigate their weaknesses. The willingness to self-assess diligently and truthfully is an essential characteristic of leadership.

This might sound like common sense, but the difference between a leader and would-be leaders is often the degree to which they purposefully seek to understand who they are and how they are perceived. In the leadership academies conducted by one of the authors, almost all teachers and staff members at the beginning claim to be "self-aware."

These teachers and staff members claim to know their abilities and growth areas, and to know how they are perceived. However, many of them have created their views or assessment of themselves without actively seeking feedback from subordinates and supervisors on a regular basis. One solid way of gaining an appropriate ability to assess one's self is asking for feedback and taking it to heart.

One Principal's Story of A Successful Effort at Leadership

Kathy was the principal of a middle school in Colorado Springs. Among the many things she did to get accurate feedback on her performance as a leader was to convene a *Principal Evaluation Committee*. The committee comprised teachers and support staff; some of her harshest critics were included. They conducted surveys, interviewed teachers, and used a rigorous rubric to assess the principal. They then reviewed their evaluation and critiqued the principal in a two-hour "post conference."

When her colleagues asked her why she subjected herself to such scrutiny, she replied that her staff was the best judge of how she was performing, noting also that the District evaluation she received was not useful (as hardly anyone from the District office ever came by to see her). Teachers can also seek honest feedback about their own abilities as a leader from other teachers acting as mentors and even from parents who are willing to share their honest views with the teacher.

One of the authors, in 1972, created the first computer-assisted student evaluation of faculty at a university in the United States. Students were asked a series of questions about each faculty member they had, including questions about the faculty member's ability to lead, and the student responses became an integral part of the university's decision whether to grant tenure or not. Therefore, students may also be a valuable source of feedback to teachers at certain grade levels.

Unfortunately, in many schools and districts, instructional feedback or constructive criticism on job performance is rarely given. Evaluations are often done perfunctorily and the evaluations rarely, if ever, touch on leadership strengths and weaknesses. Consequently, many teachers will have to create their own feedback systems to help them assess their own leadership strengths and weaknesses. Teachers must find some way to get a clear understanding of their talents, preferences, and potential. Researched-based personality inventories or instruments may help.

Self-Assessment and Having Others Assess You

Exercise 1:

Rate yourself from one to ten on each of the following ten questions. Then ask others you know to rate you on these ten questions and compare the scores.

1. I self-identify as a leader.
2. I purposely assess my talents and preferences, using researched-based instruments to help me do so.
3. I actively seek input or feedback from subordinates and supervisors regarding my job performance.
4. I act upon the feedback in ways that reinforce my strengths and mitigate my weaknesses.
5. I am a student of leadership, understanding different leadership concepts and frameworks, and work to develop my leadership abilities.
6. I establish challenging and measurable personal goals.
7. I monitor my progress in reaching those goals.
8. I habitually reflect on my actions and my effectiveness.

9.   I purposefully assess how my actions and attitudes affect others.
10. I take action to be a positive influence in the organization.

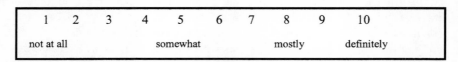

Average your scores regarding how you rated yourself and how others rated you and observe the difference between the scores others give you and you give yourself.

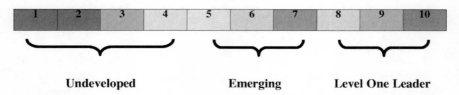

Then ask yourself the questions. . . .

• What actions can I take to improve my scores that I gave myself and others gave me so that I can become a better level one leader?

    1. _____

    2. _____

    3. _____

    4. _____

    5. _____

• What can other school teachers and school leaders do to help me improve the scores I gave myself and others gave me so that I can become a better level one leader?

    1. _____

    2. _____

3. _____

4. _____

5. _____

End of Exercise 1.

This leadership exercise done in a nonthreatening manner allows and even encourages teachers to seek honest feedback from others to get a more accurate picture of how they are perceived as leaders and how they operate as leaders. The feedback which teachers give themselves and receive from others must be requested in an atmosphere that promotes everyone giving their honest opinion, with absolutely no retribution or negative consequences for even the harshest criticism.

Teachers may share the results of this exercise with others, but it is not essential to do this to get substantial benefit from this exercise. Teachers who get constructive feedback and study it will have an enhanced ability to assess themselves properly, act on their strengths, and seek to improve their weaknesses.

Reflect

Securing feedback from others is important as shown above. Leaders also give themselves feedback and use this feedback to improve themselves through careful reflection. Self-assessment can be informal and take place weekly or at regular intervals. Informally, teachers can continually review their job performance and reflect to determine if they were being a successful leader or not in that instance, identify the lessons they learned from that instance, and develop their own leadership development exercises to make progress where they have identified weaknesses.

In each instance where a teacher evaluates or reflects on how successful or unsuccessful they were in attempting to provide leadership, the teacher must be very honest and assess the impact their actions had, positive and negative, on others and the organization.

A second leadership exercise to help teachers assess themselves in the area of leadership could take place weekly or monthly along the following lines:

Exercise 2:

During the past week (month) I had the following opportunities to lead and help myself and others achieve a goal or create and fulfill an opportunity:

1. _____

2. _____

3. _____

4. _____

5. _____

Of the five opportunities, I took the opportunity to be a leader: _____ (number of times)

The reasons in the other opportunities why I did not seize the opportunity to become a leader were:

1. _____

2. _____

3. _____

4. _____

5. _____

My specific leadership weakness or the negative consequences I was concerned about which I used as an excuse not to lead when I had the opportunity to lead include:

1. _____

2. _____

3. _____

4. _____

5. _____

When I did lead, I was successful because:

1. _____

2. _____

3. _____

4. _____

5. _____

When I did lead, I was not successful because:

1. _____

2. _____

3. _____

4. _____

5. _____

End of Exercise 2.

Exercises 1 and 2 should be done in writing, and the record of these exercises with the date the exercise was undertaken should be kept in a notebook or folder by the teacher. Each exercise can be done many times over one's career and yield new benefits. Keeping a leadership folder, three-ring binder, or some other type of notebook, or keeping these exercises on your computer and numbering the exercises each time you do them, such as "Exercise 1 Second time" or some other naming convention, should prove to be very useful for any teacher who seeks to become a better leader.

Self assessment is a great starting point in becoming a successful leader. Leaders at the level one stage are purposeful about being reflective and conducting well researched assessments about themselves, the environment, and all those who can assist them or impede them in solving the problem at hand or the opportunity that is presented.

Level one leaders establish individual, measurable goals and monitor their progress in reaching those goals. They challenge themselves to improve and grow and benefit from their ever improving ability to assess themselves, and see their own strengths as their calling to be a leader and see their weaknesses as their limitations to be a better leader. They surround themselves with people who have strengths in areas where they have weaknesses.

Level Two Leadership

Level two leadership focuses on how leaders understand others and how they understand their environment. Level two leaders have developed their skills in the area of perspective. Their leadership abilities allow them to have a greater impact on others and the organization than those who do not understand others or the environments in which they seek to lead. Teachers who understand their students, the parents with whom they deal, the overall school environment, will be better leaders than those who don't.

Often level two leaders can understand when leading my example will work and when it will take more than just giving others a good, solid example of leadership or performance. Level two leaders, by understanding others and their environment, will know:

- who all of the key stakeholders are for any given situation
- the best ways of communicating with each stakeholder group
- when rewards will be most beneficial
- how much accountability and oversight to build into their leadership behaviors
- whom to delegate specific tasks
- how to identify, understand, and overcome barriers to success
- how to identify and limit the impact of those most likely oppose their leadership
- how to deal effectively with resource constraints
- how to establish their leadership role early in the process
- how to deal with early setbacks effectively

In the example above, Sally could not lead the math department to success because she did not understand and predict the resistance she would receive to new, improved teaching methods, and she did not understand how entrenched the environment was in not being willing to change even though poor performance was not the goal of anyone in the department. Successful role models and mentors often exhibit level two leadership traits by doing the little things that their followers or those they are leading understand and appreciate.

Level two leaders almost always know how to assess the problem at hand. Level two leaders assess problems and challenges from the perspective of a leader, the perspective of how are we going to solve this problem, overcome this challenge, or achieve this goal. The more one seeks to understand others, the environment, the problems, challenges and opportunities, the better they become at understanding each of these elements of the environment and the more detailed and accurate their understandings become.

Level two leaders:

- assess the true nature of a problem
- investigate fully the sources of the problem
- seek to understand the full set of interrelationships and interactions impacting the problem
- attempt to understand exactly the opportunity that may present itself as a problem or challenge
- understand people's general resistance to change
- appreciate the resistance people create when change is being done "to" them instead of "with" them
- comprehend that stakeholders will fight against just about anything if they were not consulted early on in the process
- evaluate the full extent and nature of the resources it will take to resolve the problem
- estimate properly how much time it will take in a given environment to accomplish a goal or resolve a problem

Those who identify a problem and just talk about it are complainers. They are not leaders. Level two leaders assess problems and seek to understand others and the environment. Level two leaders identify solutions to problems or challenges only after understanding others and the environment. Level two leaders do this because they appreciate that only with this understanding can a leader help achieve goals on time, on budget, and with the valued assistance of others. Level two leaders want others to work with them again in trying to achieve the next goal.

Gain and Share Perspective

How often does something like the following happen in schools (or other organizations)? (Note: This is a conversation we will refer back to several times during this chapter, revising the conversation slightly to show different levels of leadership in operation).

SCENARIO 1: No leadership exhibited by either party to the conversation.

Brenda (4th grade team leader): "I heard the Curriculum Director is coming by today to observe instruction."

Tammy (colleague): "Why is she doing that?"

Brenda: "I don't know; I guess she wants to 'check up' on us."

Tammy: "I'm so tired of the mistrust. Why can't they just leave us alone to teach?"

Brenda: "Yeah, I know. Teaching's not fun anymore. Anyway, you'd better put up a lesson objective just to be safe."

Tammy: "You see—just more work!" (closing the door to her classroom)

In this instance neither Brenda nor Tammy seems to have any desire to understand exactly what is going on. However, when Brenda responds as a level two leader, the conversation could have gone on like this:

SCENARIO 2: Level Two leadership exhibited by Brenda.

Brenda: "The Curriculum Director may be coming by today to observe instruction."

Tammy: "Why is she doing that?"

Brenda: "I'm not sure, but she may want to observe how curriculum alignment is going."

Tammy: "I'm so tired of the mistrust. Why can't they just leave us alone to teach?"

Brenda: "Well, from the Curriculum Director's perspective, she needs to see if curriculum alignment is going according to plan and I understand that she wants to provide some feedback on the things this district values most—the quality of the instruction. Frankly, I find some of the feedback to be very useful."

Tammy: "Maybe. But now I have to put up lesson objectives."

Brenda: "Hey, as a team, we're making good progress with the new curriculum and it is being successful in engaging students. I'll bet she notices the progress we are making."

The key difference between the two scenarios is ***perspective***. It is one of the most fundamental qualities that separate a leader from many other employees in the school. Perspective is the willingness to see the situation from the view of others and to seek to gain a deep understanding of what is going on in the environment. The good news is that "perspective" is a skill and art that can be learned and developed. Perspective involves understanding others' points of view and understanding the interests and environment of the larger organization.

Thus, a person who is skilled at being able to develop "perspective" will listen and study others and the environment carefully to understand the thoughts, positions and interests of others, and to understand the full environment before criticizing, complaining, working against a leader who is trying to improve the situation, or attempting to act as a leader in a situation. Level two leaders always seek to understand before they seek to explain or to lead.

Accurate Perspective Requires An Accurate Assessment of the True Facts

Level two leaders conduct research, ask clarifying questions, and when they are uncertain about the environment or are not sure they understand others views and motivations, they approach them and seek out their honest points of view. They do not, like Sally did above, curtail meetings or only focus on and work with those who agree with them. They also, unlike Tammy, do not jump to conclusions like "mistrust," which Tammy assumed was the reason the curriculum director was going to visit her class. When engaging with others to find out their viewpoints and motivations, they often paraphrase others to help them clarify others' viewpoints.

Level two leaders work diligently to understand the interests of other people and groups even when, and especially when, the leader does not agree with their position. The level two leader builds relationships in order to further communication with others which fosters understanding of other points of view. The level two leader does not seek confrontation but seeks to understand fully the motivations and concerns when others confront the level two leader.

Developing one's ability to gain an accurate perspective of others' viewpoints and the environment in general allows the level two leader to avoid assumptions that turn out to be wrong, and to reserve judgment when faced with partial information or information that does not seem accurate. Likewise, level two leaders ensure they understand the goals and priorities of the larger group, of all key stakeholders and the organization as a whole. Level two leaders gain organizational perspective.

This understanding enables them to ***make sense*** of what is said by others, and the current state of policies and practices, and to be effective when they are trying to lead an organization wide activity that will require others to change the way they are currently doing things. For example, when a level two leader reads this book and tries to go into their school and get every other teacher to read this book and become a better leader, that level two leader will understand how the other teachers are doing, know which teachers will be receptive early on to the ideas of this book and which teachers will not.

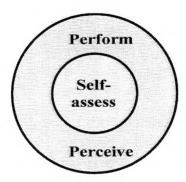

The level two leader will know that starting with the teachers who will be most receptive to the ideas and approaches of this book might be the best way to eventually get the other teaches to consider reading this book and becoming a better teacher.

Furthermore, level two leaders understand the culture and the decision-making structure in an organization. They understand that some decisions are theirs to make and some belong to someone else. They understand the best ways to influence others and the entire organization when they do not have the position power to order everyone to accept and implement the change.

Level two leaders understand that some decisions need to be made now, while other decisions, especially where there is strong disagreement, may be able to be postponed until additional information is offered or perspectives change. Timing of action, even of making a suggestion, or taking a stand, or promoting a point of view is an important element considered by all level two leaders.

Without this perspective, people are simply less effective leaders. Perspective takes time, energy, research, and patience to develop. It is indispensible to becoming a better leader. Level two leaders not only seek to develop perspective for themselves they also, like Brenda in the second version of the conversation above, seek to share their perspective with others and encourage others to develop their own perspective.

Often it is those without perspective who object out of hand to changes and improvements. While a level two leader will seek to find out their perspectives, the level two leader will also seek to convince others of their own perspective or at least guide others to see that their own perspective is reasonable and plausible, even if others do not agree with it.

Teachers As Observers—A True Strength

Teachers can be excellent level two leaders because they are such great observers. They seek to understand their students and their environment.

They promote dialogue among themselves and others. They want to see their school improve. They want to learn others' perspectives and they want others to learn their perspectives.

Teachers have all of the ingredients to become excellent at developing perspective. Teachers are highly skilled and trained in engaging in the dialogue where all parties can share their perspectives. Teachers are excellent as active listening. Teachers are gifted at searching diligently toward achieving the common goal of improving our schools.

However, most school environments are not environments where many teachers have developed strong level two leadership skills. For example, one of the authors sat in a three hour IEP (Individual Educational Plan) with the parents of a child with learning disabilities.

The principal, school psychologist, and the teachers at the IEP started off the session with the statement that the boy for whom the IEP was being developed could not perform certain tasks and mathematical assignments. The principal and teachers concluded that the boy would be removed from several classes where he was currently enrolled and put back into less advanced classes. The mother then proceeded to explain that over the past two weeks the child had become proficient at each of the tasks described above plus accomplished the mathematical assignments at home.

The principal and the teachers then repeated that the child could not perform the tasks and the mathematical assignments and they were going to remove the child from several classes.

The mother then repeated that the child was able to perform the tasks and the mathematical assignments. The mother then stated that she and her child were very proud of the boy's recent accomplishments in these areas. The mother then suggested that the principal and teachers could retest the child on the tasks and assignments. She also explained that the child worked very hard to be able to do them, showed his brothers and fellow students in those classes his work, and for the first time in the entire year was very happy to be at school, in those particular classes, and was gaining confidence.

The principal and the teachers said that the decision had already been made and the child would be removed from the classes where those tasks and math assignments were at issue.

After several hours of dialogue, the teachers, the school psychologist, and the principal reluctantly agreed to retest the child. They retested the child. The child performed the assignments, stayed in the classes, and did very well the rest of the year.

Clearly the principal, the teachers and the school psychologist were not acting as level two leaders initially. There were not willing or capable of listening carefully and gaining the perspective they needed to lead the situation properly. Finally, after the parent totally refused to give into the poor leadership and poor decision making of the teachers, the principal, and the school psychologist, the school personnel made the right decision to let the child retake the tests and to see if the mother was accurate in her assessment of her child's ability.

In this situation, a level two leader would have:

- come to the conclusion to retest the child within minutes of the beginning of the meeting after the mother asserted the child could perform the tasks in question
- would have wanted to know the accurate facts as they existed at the time of the meeting, not two weeks before.
- would not have alienated the mother, but rather worked with her as a partner
- would not have made such a great effort to stand their ground on a decision that was based on inaccurate information that was several weeks old and out of date
- would have given great weight to the importance of the mother's viewpoint
- would have given great weight to the potential harm to the child of a wrong decision based on inaccurate information
- would have apologized to the mother after the mother's view was proven accurate

Teachers Strive for Excellence

Level two leader often lead by example. Not only must level two leaders have perspective, but like a leader at any level or one who seeks to be a leader, they must also be competent. Few will or should follow an incompetent person for long. All leaders must be able to identify both competence and incompetence and label them accordingly. Leaders must be able to identify them in other teachers properly so they will know how to delegate tasks and responsibilities appropriately to those who exhibit competence.

Level two leaders must be able to discern accurate information from inaccurate information because in seeking to do research to evaluate an environment in which they wish to lead, they will be told and will uncover accurate and inaccurate information and must be able to discern the difference. Leaders must know whose information to trust and whose contradictory information to discount or throw out. They must know who is credible and a good source of information, and who is not in each situation.

Level two leaders must work hard and do the necessary research to make sure that they are correct when they accept some evidence or statements as being accurate and reject contradictory evidence or statements as being inaccurate. We would like to think that in schools everyone is competent and everyone provides accurate information all of the time. This is not so.

Teachers who are leaders must identify incompetence, whether it is at the teacher level, staff level, principal level, school superintendent level, or at the school board level. Everyone who is a leader must take a stand against incompetence in PreK–12 education, and seek to have persons in the school currently performing at levels below established competency standards, improve significantly in a reasonable amount of time.

Teachers who are leaders must strive for excellence and successfully urge others in the organization to strive for excellence at every opportunity. Organizations cannot achieve and maintain excellence if many in the organization do not actively strive for excellence and improvement. Teachers who are leaders set standards for themselves. But, as a teacher moves to the level three and level four levels, they also must seek to help set standards for everyone in the school and administration, including their peers, supervisors, and their subordinates.

Thus, it is incumbent on teachers who seek to be level three and level four leaders, as described below, to identify those in the school who are not seeking to achieve excellence and address this issue in an appropriate manner. Leaders, at all levels, assist others in improving their performance significantly.

The level two leader's pursuit of excellence and growth for themselves is not fleeting. Level two leaders are life-long learners who continue to grow personally and professionally, taking advantage of learning opportunities. These leaders constantly share their knowledge and insights, and seek to help themselves improve through life-long learning. Level two leaders care about achieving excellence in every category where they are measured. The following self-assessment at level two can assist a teacher evaluate his or her current thinking regarding level two leadership.

Self-assessment—Level Two Leadership

Level two leadership focuses on how leaders understand others. Level two leaders have perspective and competence. Their leadership abilities allow them to have a greater impact on others and the organization. This is the level educators are operating at when people describe them as leading by example.

People who are role models or mentors often exhibit level two leadership traits.

Exercise 3:
Rate yourself from one to ten on each of the following ten questions. Then ask others you know to rate you on these ten questions and compare the scores.

1. I actively attempt to obtain others' points of view and to understand their interests.
2. When faced with partial information, I reserve judgment.
3. I build relationships to further understanding.
4. I understand the goals and priorities of the organization.
5. I coordinate closely and in a timely manner with people in the organizational levels above and below me.
6. I communicate well and help others make sense of policies and practices.
7. I know what distinguished performance looks like and my view of distinguished performance matches those of other leaders in the organization.
8. I strive for excellence, helping to define excellence for my colleagues and subordinates.
9. I am a life-long learner and continue to grow professionally and to develop my craft.
10. I share my knowledge and expertise with others in the field.

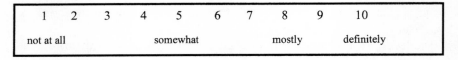

Average your scores regarding how you rated yourself and how others rated you and observe the difference between the scores others give you and you give yourself.

Average your scores.

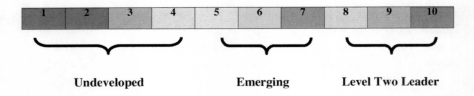

Then ask yourself the questions. . . .

- What actions can I take to improve my scores that I gave myself and others gave me so that I can be a better level two leader?

  1. _____

  2. _____

  3. _____

  4. _____

  5. _____

- What can other school teachers and school leaders do to help me improve the scores I gave myself and others gave me so that I can become a better level two leader?

  1. _____

  2. _____

  3. _____

  4. _____

  5. _____

End of Exercise 3.

Level Three Leadership

As described above, level one leaders are willing to assess their leadership strengths and weaknesses, but may not have much impact on bringing resources or people together to help resolve challenges or chart a new course toward school improvement. Level two leaders are more aware of their environment and often have a greater impact on situations because they understand the stakeholder landscape, the overall environment, they demand excellence on a regular basis, and people will follow their example.

Level three leaders are willing to take on larger and larger leadership roles as they seek to improve themselves and the overall situation as they observe it. Level one and level two leaders are centered on more passive characteristics—reflection, reserving judgment, gaining perspective, life-long learning, and while they may seek to help others improve, they have not yet fully developed a key defining characteristic of level three leaders.

It is at level three where the leader through a combination of self-knowledge, understanding, perspective, timing, and effective action, is truly able to help others and improve the immediate situation as viewed by the leader. It is the element of *effective action* and often *well-coordinated action* directed toward not only improving the situation but also helping others solve problems that distinguishes level three leadership. Level three leaders not only reach their goals and fulfill the opportunities they see, they also help others define and reach the goals others seek to achieve.

It is level three leaders who actually know how:

- to get others to improve
- to get others to become leaders
- to get others to begin to look for solutions to the challenges and problems they encounter
- to get others to act in a manner that improves the entire environment in which they work
- to begin to form effective teams
- to gain support from others to assist the leader in reaching his or her goals

Level three has numerous disciplines that are practiced and refined to a high level. They include coaching, mentoring, and team formation. Level three leaders:

- demand and receive excellence not only in themselves but also in those they lead
- are always attempting to improve themselves and all those around them
- seek to help others prepare for the next level of leadership
- define challenges and problems precisely so that others can see the challenge or problem clearly
- seek to assist others at being expert at their craft
- seek to get those who are incompetent to improve rapidly or move on to some profession or area of work where they can be at least competent
- are action oriented
- inspire and help both themselves and those they lead to maximize their human potential

Motivate

In many ways, we ask teachers to be level three leaders every day. Every day teachers motivate students and seek to help maximize students' potential. Many teachers succeed at this admirably. Similarly, we are all familiar with the athletic coach model—the person who inspires and "gets the most out of a person." These are certainly examples of level three leadership. But effective leaders are not just leaders of students and athletes, they are leaders among their colleagues and employees of the organization, even their superiors.

A level three leader who is a teacher is effective at:

- leading other teachers to be the best teacher and the best leader that teacher could be
- communicating in a manner and take deliberate actions to inspire their colleagues and those with whom they work to become excellent school employees and excellent leaders themselves
- working with their fellow teachers to set and reach high goals
- having strong aspirations for themselves, other teachers, the students they lead, and all employees of the school

Level three leaders who are teachers work hard to accomplish more using their leadership skills. For example, they seek to:

- find the time to work closely with parents to help them set the highest reasonable expectations for the best academic and extracurricular achievement their children can achieve
- enroll and encourage action by others and lead others to develop a very strong commitment to help reach goals and even help shape the goals themselves
- demonstrate personal conviction toward the success of their fellow teachers, other employees of the organization and students
- show enthusiasm for the actions they are taking and others are taking toward setting and achieving goals

Level three leaders in working with others:

- encourage greatness in people and in the schools where they work
- deal with others effectively, highlighting their strengths while diplomatically addressing and helping them address their weaknesses
- provide leadership opportunities for others
- help others set challenging, yet attainable, goals

- recognize and acknowledge others successfully and meaningfully for good performance and leadership
- develop camaraderie among staff members
- keep everyone informed in a truthful manner about their successes and failures in helping address a problem or in reaching a goal

Inspiring others and securing their commitment to the goals can be tough work. Level three leadership isn't easy, but the rewards in terms of life's satisfactions are enormous. Teachers are level three leaders in their classrooms day in and day out. Teachers can be level three leaders assisting other teachers and school administrators on a regular basis become both better teachers and better leaders.

In the example above with Brenda and Tammy, Brenda in the second scenario of the conversation demonstrated perspective and sense-making—level two leadership skills on the par of Brenda. Brenda would not have had to go much farther for her to demonstrate level three leadership and actually help Tammy in a significant way. The scenario below gives us an example of how this could have been done.

Scenario 3:

Brenda: "The Curriculum Director may be coming by today to observe instruction."

Tammy: "Why is she doing that?"

Brenda: "I'm not sure, but she may want to observe how curriculum alignment is going."

Tammy: "I'm so tired of the mistrust. Why can't they just leave us alone to teach?"

Brenda: "Well, from her perspective, she is providing some feedback on the things this district values most—the quality of the instruction. Frankly, I find some of the feedback to be very useful."

Tammy: "Maybe. But now I have to put up lesson objectives."

Brenda: "Hey, as a team, we're making good progress on those and your objectives are solid. And I'll review two of those student-response strategies with you next period if you want. Maybe if both of us look at them together, we can improve on them. So, if anyone gets a visit, I hope it's you—you'll do us proud."

With just a few words of encouragement and acknowledgement of what Tammy was doing well, plus the offer of support, in a timely manner, Brenda turned Tammy's complaint in a "leadership moment." As Brenda moves from a level two leader—one who leads by example—to a level three coach, she becomes a stronger leader who has a greater impact. Finding and creating these leadership moments when others do not see them, is a hallmark of the level three leader.

Teachers are better than just about anyone at spotting a teachable moment. Therefore, teachers are also uniquely suited to recognize leadership moments. As teachers strive to attain level three leadership competency, they improve their ability to identify and act effectively when level three leadership moments arise. Teachers can also attain level three leadership in situations dealing with parents, as challenging as that can be. Teachers who set the goal and are effective in helping parents become more active in the education of their children, are true level three leaders. Level three leaders pride themselves in being prepared and willing to act as a level three leader every time a level three opportunity arises. Level three leaders constantly look for an opportunity to lead.

Engender Trust

In order to inspire or motivate, leaders must engender and maintain trust in individuals and especially in groups. Books, doctoral theses, and thousands of articles have been written about trust. For the level three leader, trust comes down to consistency of word and deed. Level three leaders "walk their talk." Level three leaders are operationally transparent, meaning that their colleagues, subordinates, and superiors understand their actions and the rationale for their actions.

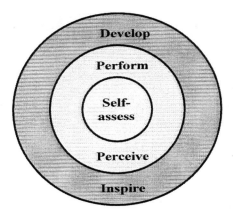

This transparency enables colleagues, other employees, administrators, and even students, to see that goals set, problems identified, and decisions made by level three leaders who are teachers are based on not only the leader's interests but also on the careful consideration of the interests of all stakeholders and the school itself. Level three leaders always have the interests of the organization in mind. Level three leaders have objectives and things they want to see accomplished, so they do have an agenda; they just don't have a *hidden* agenda.

Level three leaders must make sure they are trusted and when someone does not have full trust in a level three leader, that leader should find this out and deal with it directly, not as a confrontation, but as an opportunity to share perspectives so that trust will naturally flow from others to the level three leader and from the level three leader to those with whom the level three leader works. Trust is an essential component in level three leadership. In a leadership development session with Volunteers of America New Orleans chapter led by one of the co-authors, each person was asked to define leadership. One person defined leadership as "trust."

Trust is destroyed, sometimes permanently, by being vindictive, manipulative or deceitful. Level three leaders do not exhibit any of these behaviors. They listen to and respect the "loyal opposition." They do not take criticism or opposition personally. They use a calm, problem-solving approach when faced with a challenge or opposition. The level three leader helps create and follows agreed-upon norms for working collaboratively, and promotes everyone else getting their actual agenda out on the table for all to see and understand. Level three leaders seek cooperation even in the face of disagreement.

The phrase, "storming, norming and forming" means that in the initial phase of defining a problem, or even developing a strategy for seeking to address the problem or challenge, disagreements are encouraged. As the discussion moves along, and more facts are gathered, and more perspectives are shared, the definition of the problem and the establishment of the proper goal should become clearer. As this occurs, everyone in the process has a duty to seek to work together to develop a concise definition of the problem and a plan to resolve the problem.

Everyone need not agree on every step, but everyone should agree that they will work toward the successful implementation of the plan once it is adopted by the group or school. In the forming stage, where the solution is formed, level three leaders must seek to set up systems of fair and timely decision making. Level three leaders in the performing stage are responsible for everyone rowing in the same direction to the best of their ability once the direction is determined.

Achieving consensus is a desirable goal, but consensus does not mean unanimous consent. It does mean that everyone will work honestly toward the goal that the majority, or a super majority if so required, agrees is the best goal and the best approach to the goal. A level three leader engenders trust by promoting collaborative agreements and having them executed to the best of the abilities of everyone in the organization.

Maximize Potential

Like any good coach, level three leaders are successful at maximizing human potential. They help others develop. They find ways to connect each person's talents and passion to the work. Level three leaders identify strengths and weaknesses and find out about a person's dreams or individual goals. Then level three leaders help the person address their weaknesses and tap those strengths to provide opportunities for their goals to be realized.

The example below from a school setting demonstrates how a level three does this.

Dale, who was a middle school principal, once supervised a teacher, Bob, who was competent, but seemed to have lost his original passion for teaching students. Alone with him in the teachers' lounge one day, Dale asked Bob what he hoped to be doing five years from now. Bob said he didn't know and admitted that he felt "a little stuck." Dale then asked Bob to just dream a little and to think of something he would really like to do that was within the realm of the possible.

Bob responded by saying that he had always thought he could do a great job as a curriculum director and that he was already coaching some of his colleagues on alignment and instructional strategies. Being a level three leader, Dale began to think of a way to combine Bob's classroom abilities with his goal of being a curriculum director. Dale began to think of how to do this and do it in a manner that would promote the school's goal of raising student achievement significantly.

Bob and Dale worked out a plan for Bob to begin to do spot observations with him twice a week during Bob's planning period. The following year, Dale made Bob an instructional coach. Bob then began coursework to earn an administrator's license. Bob's passion returned as he got to develop level three leadership skills. As a result, other teachers improved, student outcomes improved, and the quality of Bob's work, the quality of his life, and Bob's level of enthusiasm improved immensely.

Of course, maximizing potential is not synonymous with getting a different or higher level position. In the Harrison School District in Colorado Springs, teachers and support staff attend a leadership academy to strengthen their leadership skills and abilities. There is no intent or attempt made in the program to encourage teachers or staff to become administrators. The objective is to build leadership capability by providing an opportunity for teachers and staff to discover and develop their leadership talents and style, and give them key insights, strategies and leadership development tools.

For all teachers who aspire to level three leadership, taking leadership development courses can provide direction and encouragement to assist other teachers at every opportunity to become better teachers and better leaders.

Teachers can also read books, undertake exercises and learn much of what is needed for effective level leadership on the job. As a person begins to undertake level three leadership, feedback will be forthcoming, we can assure you. Level three leadership is just as important for a teacher who wants to become more effective in the classroom and to help improve the school at the same time, as it is for anyone who wants to be a principal.

Exercise 4:

For the level three leadership exercise, think of a teacher with whom you do not have a close relationship. You have heard some complaints about this teacher's ability to teach and you understand that the student outcomes are not good for this teacher's classes. As a level three leader, develop and implement a strategy to approach and be successful in helping this teacher improve. Repeat this exercise as often as you can with other teachers and let teachers know they can come to you for advice. Write down your strategy, what you did, what worked and what did not work, and, if you can, track any improvements that the teacher whom you have assisted may have achieved.

End of Exercise 4.

Level Four Leadership

The first three levels of leadership operate primarily at the level of self and others, with others being individuals. The next level of leadership, level four leadership, is where a leader:

- can help lead and engage an entire organization to become aligned
- assists the entire school work together as a group or team
- helps shape and get others to buy into a shared vision for the school or district
- assists the school and all stakeholders develop solid plans to reach school goals
- takes leadership and organizing roles in implementing strategies and plans
- has the goal of not just improving the school, but also transforming the entire organization's capabilities and outlook.

Level four leaders:

- help shape the identity of organizations
- help secure the long-term success of the organization

- help improve the reputation of the organization and how others perceive it
- help increase the positive expectations of everyone who deals with the school.

The activities of a level four leader are mutually reinforcing and operate at the organizational level. We call this leadership *at every step.*

There are several key roles for teachers to be level four leaders in their schools and in their lives outside of schools. Level four leaders uplift an entire class of students. Level four leaders who are teachers set and achieve such high standards that they affect the standards and goals of other teachers. Level four leaders who are teachers affect the way the school administrators, principals, parents, and others treat and interact with teachers and the entire school environment. Level four leaders who are teachers say:

- "This is my school and we are going to make it better."
- "This is my school and we are going to improve student outcomes—grades and graduation rates."
- "This is my school and we are going to end cheating."
- "This is my school and we are going to reduce absenteeism."
- "This is my school and we are going to change the system that has students only have classes a few hours a day during an eight hour school day which encourages students to leave the school and go off campus during the school day."

Level four leaders are constant advocates for their peers. Level four teachers say:

- "This is my school and our teachers will have all of the supplies they need for their classrooms and will not have to pay out of their small salaries for supplies they need."
- "This is my school and teachers will be listened to by principals about what is best for the school because we have great ideas for improving the school."
- "This is my school and we will get all of our teachers to work together to improve our school."

Teachers who operate or want to operate as level four leaders know that statements like these are just as much the province of teachers as they are the province of school superintendents or principals. When a teacher takes a stand for the entire school, or all other teachers, that teacher is beginning to act as a level four leader. As the teacher becomes more proficient in helping the school move successfully toward significant, school wide improvements, that teacher is operating as a seasoned level four leader.

Create a Shared Vision

Level four leaders who are teachers help create, foster, and support a shared vision for their school. They help gain support of other teachers to support, nurture and refine this vision. They help create an environment where every teacher is always seeking improvement within the school and a better reputation for the school. Level four leaders who are teachers never view themselves as mere cheerleaders or promoters of their school. They are, in their eyes, a key member of the team that makes the school as effective as it can be.

Once a vision or set of goals is adopted by the school with substantial teacher input, level four leaders who are teachers help translate this vision into real plans and measurable goals over the short term so progress, or lack of progress, can be assessed on a regular basis. Level four leaders invite accountability. Level four leaders help achieve clarity and focus in schools by helping set standards, benchmarks and goals for their schools. Certainly the best principals should be level four leaders. But an equal or better argument can be made that for schools to reach their full potential, teachers must become level four leaders as well.

Transcend The Organization

The goal of level four leaders is to have every person, resource and element of the organization jell together, plan together, work together, and dream together, so that the vision and goals of the organization transcend the organization itself and take on greater and greater meaning in each participant's life. While the organization can and will have setbacks, once the vision has transcended the organization, that vision will remain steadfast among leaders and followers and will guide all in the organization to overcome barriers or right the ship.

Every school and every educational effort is part of our nation's goal and mission to give each and every individual the best opportunities for the best life possible. Each school is part of the whole, the American dream. Each school can help open doors for its students and has a duty to the students and our nation to do so. Each school must work as hard as possible to have all of the resources, financial and otherwise, to meet the educational needs of its students. Each school must know of its central role in America being as great as it can be.

Visions, if they are to guide an institution or organization, do not change much over time. They are refined and improved, but they are never sold out. They are not applicable only on some days and not others, or some groups of students, and not others. They are the glue that holds the organization together, has people work together, and has the greatest impact on how the organization touches the lives of all those associated with the organization. The vision for a school is not the province of merely the principal or a school superintendent. It is the province of each teacher, even those who have only just started teaching there.

The vision for a school is also the province of the students who attend there, as well as teachers and administrators. It is the students' and the teachers' shared vision that their school will be the best academic or athletic or artistic or vocational or special needs school it can be that is essential for that school to be true to that vision. For a school to realize its vision that it be safe, academically sound, athletically strong, artistically gifted, every key stakeholder in the school from students, parents, teachers, staff, principals, and other supporters of the school including alumni, must share that vision.

Level four leaders create and support a shared vision. They work every day toward keeping that vision alive, making real progress toward that vision, instilling that vision into every person whose life is touched by the school. Level four leaders who are teachers serve as exemplary representatives of the school and its vision. They show the world that the vision is being made real every day and improvements toward realizing that vision are being undertaken every day.

Maintain And Demand Integrity

Level four leaders maintain not only their integrity but the integrity of others and the organization itself at all times, especially when the going gets rough. They stop the backstabbing that represents a common form of lack of integrity in educational institutions. They stop backstabbing, first by catching it, all of it, or at least most of it, as it happens. This is no easy task. Then, they stop it by acknowledging it, its harm to the organization, and showing to everyone in the organization that they will not tolerate it.

Level four leaders defend their organizations from outside attacks and inside attacks, that can be likened to "friendly fire" in the battlefield. Friendly fire is the unintentional harm that a person on one side of a fight does to another person on the same side of the fight. Like in the military, in organizations and educational institutions, friendly fire can be deadly.

Level four leaders know not only how to recognize friendly fire in all of its permutations, they know when the conditions are starting to exist that promote or predict friendly fire. They see the handwriting on the wall and they take action, quickly and decisively, to prevent harmful attacks from outside of an organization and from friendly fire within an organization as well. Level four leaders cut little slack for those who actions, knowingly or unknowingly, are keeping the school from reaching its true potential.

Level four leaders:

- speak the truth to all and have no fear when they speak the truth
- demand that all speak the truth to power and peers

- set high, but achievable standards
- acknowledge successes and failures
- do not allow for excuses
- do not tolerate mere or idle complaints without action to address the problem
- always work hard to understand the reasons for failure

Level four leaders also:

- maintain integrity
- seek and disseminate only facts that are accurate
- never tolerate false statements about others in their school
- provide honest feedback and welcome honest feedback

Level four leaders know that every stakeholder group involved in schools and education is important. They acknowledge the key role and valuable input of every stakeholder group of the school, even when they oppose the position of the stakeholder group. Level four leaders seek to defuse situations that pit students against teachers or principals, parents against teachers or principals, or one stakeholder against another.

Level four leaders know that every stakeholder's commitment to and participation in the improvement of the school is essential. Level four leaders seek to expand the number of stakeholders who want to contribute positively to their schools and helping the school achieve its vision. When children of parents who are alumni of a PreK–12 school also become students at that school, these parents are often very active supporters of the school.

Yet, alumni, even if their children are not going to the PreK–12 school, or they do not have children, can be enrolled to be a very supportive stakeholder group, and teachers acting as level four leaders can play a substantial role in working with these alumni to be strong supporters of the school. Alumni can be supportive of a PreK–12 school even if they no longer live in the same community. They need to be recruited and enrolled, and teachers can be of great assistance working with administrators and staff, in this effort.

Level four leaders seek to gain the support and positive involvement of the largest number of stakeholders possible into school improvement processes. When this planning for inclusion of stakeholders is done well, then teachers can play a very important role as ambassadors to, and leaders and supporters of, every stakeholder group that wants to make a positive impact in the school environment.

Exercise 5:

For the lever four leadership exercise, think of a school-wide problem or challenge that you would like to see resolved, or a school wide opportunity that you would like to see fulfilled. Get clear what your own strengths and weaknesses are as a leader and subject matter expert in dealing with this situation. Then study who is doing what on this matter and how different groups are taking different stands on the issue or are staying out of this issue entirely. Then begin to discuss with others your ideas for how to improve the situation and encourage them to take leadership roles in helping resolve the situation.

Then, as a level four leader, announce to the school in an appropriate manner that you are taking a stand that you are willing to lead the effort to resolve this situation or fulfill this opportunity. Touch base with every stakeholder group and secure their positive involvement in the development of the goal, the gathering of necessary resources, the scheduling, and development of the strategy and implementation approach to resolving this challenge.

Keep track of what everyone is doing to reach the goal, acknowledge all participants, monitor progress, identify challenges and develop strategies to deal with each important challenge, and lead your school to achieving this goal. Keep a separate notebook or folder on this exercise. You can repeat this exercise as often as you find school-wide problems or challenges where you are willing to accept leadership roles. As you lead, and certainly when this leadership activity has concluded, ask and answer the following questions:

• What actions could I have taken to improve my leadership in this project?

1. _____

2. _____

3. _____

4. _____

5. _____

• What else have I learned about leadership as a result of my acting in a leadership role regarding this school wide challenge?

1. _____

2. _____

3. _____

4. _____

5. _____

- What do I need to learn or what skills do I need to develop to be a better leader?

  1. _____

  2. _____

  3. _____

  4. _____

  5. _____

- What have I done in this leadership activity that has helped others either become better leaders or be more willing themselves to step forward as leaders the next time a school challenge comes about?

  1. _____

  2. _____

  3. _____

  4. _____

  5. _____

End of Exercise 5.

SUMMARIZING THE FOUR LEVELS OF LEADERSHIP

Below, we summarize the four levels of leadership that are applicable to teachers in every school in America and in every home school situation. Each level of leadership can play a pivotal role in improving student outcomes, teacher satisfaction, teacher longevity, and promote teacher excellence. Effective leadership on the part of teachers can improve the reputation of our schools, improve the funding of our schools, and improve student and teacher morale and enthusiasm in our schools. Further, improved leadership by teachers can improve and maintain safety, and improve the general public's willingness to contribute to, volunteer for, and support the best possible education for the children.

The four levels of leadership are combined into the following: ***Leadership Rubric.***

Table 2.1   Leadership Rubric

LEVEL ONE *(Self-assess)*			
Key Action	*Basic*	*Effective*	*Distinguished*
Self-assesses	The teacher either identifies him or herself as a leader or as a person who wants to become a leader. The teacher participates in leadership development training. The teacher participates in exercises and personality inventories that help **assess personal talents and preferences**. Level one leaders understand their job descriptions, but are often unclear of their full role in achieving the goals of the organization. The teacher welcomes feedback, but sometimes discounts feedback that outlines areas for improvement and spurs additional feedback the leader does not like.	The teacher **assesses personal strengths, areas for growth, and preferences** by using researched-based instruments to assess talents and preferences (i.e. Myers-Briggs, FIRO-B, Teacher Insight). The leader seeks to understand and promote an impactful role in the organization and outlines specific actions that will help fulfill this role. The leader **actively seeks input** or feedback from subordinates and supervisors in order to get a more accurate picture of how others perceive the leader. This person **self-identifies** as a leader.	The leader **assesses personal strengths, areas for growth, and preferences and** uses researched-based instruments to help promote a high level of self-assessment. The leader **actively seeks input** or feedback from subordinates and supervisors in order to get a more accurate picture of others' perceptions. The leaders **acts upon the feedback** in ways that reinforce strengths and mitigates weaknesses and becomes a diligent **student of leadership**, understanding different models and frameworks. The leader attempts to develop new leadership abilities and is successful in having others identify him or herself as a leader.

LEVEL TWO (Perceive)			
Key Action	*Basic*	*Effective*	*Distinguished*
Seeks to understand perspective of others	The teacher seeks to understand others and **builds relationships** to further that understanding. The leader **listens**, but may not seek to understand fully those around the leader and their motivations. The leader's interests and point of view are always paramount and tries to convince others before the leader understands the points of view of others.	The teacher **listens well** in order to understand first before the leader tries to make others understand his or her point of view. In conversations, the leader asks clarifying questions and actively attempts to fully underrstand **others' points of view** and understand their interests. When faced with partial information, judgment is **reserved**. The leader consistently **builds relationships** to further understanding.	The teacher **uses active listening** strategies and actively attempts to get **others' points of view** and understand their interests. The leader tries to determine the talents and preferences of others and engages individuals appropriately. The leader makes decisions in a timely manner, and not prematurely. The leader seeks out opposing voices. The leader consistently **builds relationships** to further understanding.

| Gains organizational perspective | The teacher **understands the goals and priorities** of the organization. However, this level leader does not act in either a strong or decisive way to help achieve those goals. This leader has a narrow perspective of organizational effectiveness, focusing on his or her own interests and duties. | The teacher **understands the goals and priorities** of the organization and works hard to understand the role others play in serving the organization. The leader ensures **timely and close coordination** with people in the organizational levels above and below him or her. The leader understands and helps other **make sense of policies and practices** of the organization, whether the leader agrees with them or not. When this level leader disagrees with a policy, he or she begins to take action to change the policy. | The teacher **understands the goals and priorities** of the organization and understands the role others play in serving the organization. This leader **understands the decision-making structure** and knows which decisions he or she can and should influence, can make on his or her own, and which decisions belong to others. The leader ensures **timely and close coordination** with people in the organizational levels above and below him. The leader helps other **make sense of policies and practices** of the organization. |

LEVEL TWO (Perform)			
Key Action	Basic	Effective	Distinguished
Strives for excellence	These teachers try to do the **best work they can do**. They do not work according to a strict time schedule, but do what it takes to get the job done well. However, they may not know what distinguished performance looks like. This level of leader is sometimes stymied by obstacles to mission accomplishment because they are not capable of enrolling the entire organization behind their goals or projects.	These teachers **understand the various "levels of quality"operating around them** and know what distinguished performance looks like. They do not work according to a strict time schedule, but do what it takes to get the job done well. They are not perfectionists, but try to be **experts at their craft**. When faced with obstacles, this level of leader nonetheless finds a way to meet individual or organizational goals.	These teachers **understand "levels of quality,"** know what distinguished performance looks like and **help define excellence** for colleagues and subordinates. They do not work according to a strict time schedule, but do what it takes to get the job done well. They are not perfectionists, but try to be **experts at their craft**. When faced with obstacles, they nonetheless find a way to meet a goal. This level of leader is a **creative problem solver** and takes advantage of **group synergy** to maximize effectiveness.

| **Continues to learn** | The teacher is a keen observer, reads professional literature and is a member of professional organizations. The leader attends workshops or takes continuing education classes. However, this leader does little to put into practice all that is learned or help others gain from what this person learns. There may be a gap between learning and improvement. | The teacher is a **life-long learner** and continues to grow professionally, taking advantage of learning opportunities. This leader regularly attempts to share knowledge gained with colleagues. The leader values continuing education and **stays current** in his or field of expertise and the leadership development literature. This leader applies what he or she learns to a great extent. | The teacher is a **life-long learner** and continues to grow professionally, taking advantage of learning opportunities. The leader **demonstrates growth** in many areas. This leader regularly **shares knowledge gained**, affecting positively the attitude of others toward lifelong learning. The leader values continuing education and **stays current** in his or her field. |

LEVEL THREE (Inspire)			
Key Action	Basic	Effective	Distinguished
Motivates	The teacher shows a positive attitude, acts consistently with the belief that the organization can improve and ultimately be successful. While the leader models having a positive attitude, this leader takes *few deliberate steps* to motivate the staff and rally them to reach shared aspirations.	The teacher takes *deliberate actions* to motivate the staff and rallies them to reach shared aspirations. The leader models the way and demonstrates *personal conviction* toward the success of students and employees of the organization. This leader shows enthusiasm for what the organization is doing – being a *cheerleader and recognizing others* for good performance and leadership.	The teacher continually motivates teachers and the staff to reach higher goals and is able to secure the teachers and staff's *commitment*. The leader models the way and demonstrates *personal conviction* toward the success of the employees and the organization, showing enthusiasm for what the organization is doing and being a *cheerleader.* The leader regularly encourages others and highlights their strengths. The leader *recognizes others* for good performance and leadership and develops camaraderie among all school employees and students.

| Engenders trust | The teacher's words and actions are largely consistent. The leader **listens** to people, and tries to address their concerns. This leader may not explain their actions fully, assuming that others will abide by the decisions the leader makes or goals the leader sets. This type of leader is not easily approachable and does not form cohesive teams or devote the time necessary to have others develop a strong understanding of the leader's motivations. | Through **consistency** of word and deed, the teacher engenders trust. The leader is operationally **transparent**, and others understand most, if not all of the leader's decisions and actions. The leader listens to people and addresses their concerns, paying sincere respects the "loyal opposition." Colleagues, students, supervisors and subordinates feel they can raise issues or **confide** in the leader. The leader does not take opposition personally. | Through **consistency** of word and deed, the teacher engenders trust and is operationally **transparent. Others** understand the leader's actions and the rationale. The leader listens to people and addresses their concerns and pays sincere respect to the "loyal opposition." All stakeholders of the school assume the leader's decisions are made with **their interests** and the interests of the organization in mind. The leader does not take things personally and uses a **problem-solving approach** when faced with a challenge. The leader helps create and follows agreed-upon norms for working collaboratively. |

LEVEL THREE (Develop)			
Key Action	Basic	Effective	Distinguished
Maximizes potential	The teacher promotes and encourages others to think for themselves and have some control over their work activities. However, this person does encourage others to do anything out of the ordinary or work hard with colleagues to promote their growth. Colleagues receive little guidance from this leader.	The teacher promotes and encourages others to think for themselves and take a stand to **exert influence** over their work activities and work events. The leader provides clear direction and sets **parameters**, but encourages people to have a wide latitude to be creative in order to accomplish operational objectives. The leader encourages leadership attributes among fellow teachers and all involved with the school.	The teacher promotes and encourages others to think for themselves and take a stand to **exert influence** and have reasonable control over work events. The leader creates parameters and guidelines for operating, leaving day-to-day decisions to the front line level. The leader finds ways to connect each person's talents and passion to the work, building **leadership density** and encouraging leadership opportunities for all.

| Leads change | The teacher looks for ways to improve the organization and is receptive to new ideas. The leader tries to build acceptance to change, but may fail to communicate clear rationale or **garner support.** Change efforts may be developed without a clear idea of how it will support organizational goals. The leader does not prepare others to accept new ideas, nor builds acceptance for positive change. | The teacher continually looks for ways to improve the organization, being a promoter of and being **receptive** to new ideas and change. The leader serves as a responsible **change agent,** building acceptance to changes in proper stages by articulating sound rationale for change and implements change in ways that minimize resistance and garners support. The leader is **adaptable** and is not discouraged by things out of the leader's control. | The teacher is committed to improvement and not satisfied with the status quo. The leader **challenges** the way things have always been done, seeking more effective ways to accomplish goals and improve the organization. The leader seeks out good ideas and works to implement them, while **effecting change** in ways that secure cooperation and advance the goals of the organization. The leader is **comfortable with ambiguity**, is adaptable, and not discouraged by things out of the leader's control. |

LEVEL FOUR (Envision)			
Key Action	Basic	Effective	Distinguished
Create a shared vision	The teacher has a vision, but that vision may **not be translated into meaningful guidance** for the organization. Discussions around improving the future of the organization may not be purposeful and may not lead to organization improvement. The efforts by the leader have meaning and influence for some members of the school but do not impact or change the behavior of many in the school.	The teacher has a vision of what the organization is about and where it is going and articulates that vision in a way that **provides meaning** to others in the school and the community at large. The leader secures the enrollment of others in the school to validate a **"mission statement"** that holds meaning for most members of the organization and stakeholders and guides their behaviors.	The teacher **engages** or assists in engaging most everyone in the school in creating or maintaining a shared vision of what the organization is about and where it is going. Other teachers and staff respond positively to the leader's efforts to help develop plans and **take steps** to secure the long-term success of the organization. The leader encourages and supports all teachers, staff members, and students **working in mutually reinforcing ways** to accomplish the school's goals.

Establishes goals and clarifies purpose	The teacher helps develops general goals and standards that are focused on school improvement, but may not be compelling, measurable or gain the full support of all school stakeholders. The leader does not make the **rationale** for some goals clear to everyone in the school. School stakeholders accept the goals, but the goals **do not guide** their efforts in any meaningful way.	The teacher helps develops **measurable** goals that will improve the school and **provides focus** and clarity to the goals through **indicators of success**. All key stakeholders understand the goals and **use the goals and indicators** to guide their efforts. The organization's goals meet the requirements established by supervisory institutions.	The teacher **engages** others in the school to develop measurable goals that will improve the school. The goals are not only clear, but also directly and purposefully reinforce the school's vision. The leader **provides focus** and clarity to the goals through **indicators of success**. All stakeholders **use the goals and indicators** to guide their efforts. The organization's goals more than fulfill the requirements established by supervisory institutions and enhance the reputation of the school.

LEVEL FOUR (Serve)			
Key Action	*Basic*	*Effective*	*Distinguished*
Transcends organization	The teacher is *service oriented* and consistently acts and helps make decisions based on the needs of others and the good of the school. The leader serves the school well, but lacks commitment to something larger like being a force for the improvement of education for all PreK-12 students in America.	The teacher is *service oriented* and consistently acts and helps make decisions based on the needs of others and the good of the school. The leader makes *personal sacrifices* for the sake of the organization. The leader's notion of service transcends the organization and the teacher influences others in the school to become *committed to a cause or idea that is beyond the mere success of the school and its students.*	The teacher is *service oriented* and consistently acts and helps makes decisions based on the needs of others and the good of the school. The leader's notion of service transcends the organization as the teacher influences others to become *committed to a cause or idea.* The leader takes action to further a good cause or idea, helping others to support the larger concept or the greater good and makes *personal sacrifices* for the sake of others or the common good.

| Maintains integrity | The teacher follows accepted moral practices and ethical standards. The leader follows customs, rules, laws and policies and does what the leader thinks is expected. However, the leader's actions are guided by a calculation of tangible gains or rewards, and may not feel bound to hold others or even him or herself accountable to the highest standards of honor, loyalty, or duty. | The teacher maintains the **highest standards of personal integrity and ethics,** keeping his or her word and walking the talk. The leader does things for the **right reasons**, not because they are required by law or policy. The leader does the right things even when no one is watching or even if the leader will not receive recognition. | The teacher maintains the **highest standards of personal integrity and ethics,** keeping his or her word and walking the talk. The leader does things for the **right reasons**, not because they are required by law or policy, doing the right things even when no one is watching or even if no receive recognition will be received. The leader lives by some **code of honor, loyalty, or duty**. The leader helps others to do the right thing through exemplary behavior. |

CONCLUSION

This leadership framework gives teachers a rubric to guide their leadership education and development. It is designed to mirror reality and to assist educators in becoming better leaders. This framework is designed to help promote and manage conversations that assist teachers in developing a shared language around leadership for teachers. Using this framework, one teacher will know exactly what another teacher means when he or she says, "That leader would have been more successful if he or she had used level three leadership behaviors."

Achieving level one leadership is a very significant leadership development accomplishment. With effort and training, teachers can go from being people who think they are not leaders, to being very good level one or level two leaders in a matter of months. Each year where a person seeks to become a better leader should yield improvements in one's leadership capacity. Most leaders, after gaining leadership experience at an ever-increasing level, become better at self-assessment, perception, leading others and leading entire organizations.

Leaders must always stay in touch with each stakeholder group and consistently improve their perspective with and trust from each group. This is often where leaders fail. They often tune out and turn off those who oppose them. They fail to listen to them in any meaningful way. They fail to acknowledge them or even have a conversation with them. They eliminate the potential of ever working with them in the future, even when they agree on an issue. Understanding and managing the stakeholder process is important for leaders at every level.

Often leaders fail because they cut ethical corners because they think they can get away with it. Today, in the internet age, no leader can ever expect to get away with unethical conduct. Some leaders fail, as was the case of Sally (the person promoted to be head of the math department described at the beginning of the chapter), because they just give up and do not know how to operate at level two, three or four. Some leaders fail because they run out of steam and no longer have the energy or enthusiasm to lead or participate effectively in working on solutions and setting goals.

This chapter promotes your success in operating at any level of leadership at any time. In some situations, level one leadership will be sufficient. In other situations you will want to move to level two leadership where you devote enough time to understand everyone's perspective. In other situations you will want to assist others in becoming better leaders on this issue, a level three action. And, in some matters, you will want to undertake level four leadership and take full responsibility for leading the entire organization to achieve the desired goal.

Leaders always seek to estimate the amount of time any leadership level will take on any matter. Leaders do take on many responsibilities, but not more than they can handle. We know teachers' schedules are already very busy. But we believe as teachers become better leaders, they can fit additional leadership responsibilities into their working lives.

Leadership at levels three and four require substantial planning. Level four requires identifying and securing the necessary resources to achieve the goal or enrolling someone else who can do that to assist you in taking responsibility for achieving a solution at the organizational level. Teachers can be very effective level one, two, three or four leaders at any time in their career. Leadership does not require seniority. It requires leadership skills and leadership dedication. The remainder of this book is designed to assist teachers in gaining experience as a leader and being able to spot leadership opportunities that others may not see.

Chapter 3

Expanding Leadership Capacity

BECOMING A BETTER LEADER

A consistent theme running throughout this book is that everyone has leadership potential. We are not sure if everyone can learn to become a *great* leader, but there is strong evidence that with time and training, most people can become good, if not excellent leaders. Often, the long-term success of a significant reform or initiative in an educational institution rests on the premise that the educational institution can and will expand the leadership capabilities of its people so that the reform or initiative will be appropriately supported and led over the long run.

In the past, the focus in PreK–12 schools has been primarily on training and improving the leadership capacity of principals, assistant principals, and top administrators of an educational institution. This book and this chapter stake the bold claim that in order to expand the leadership capacity of an educational institution to its fullest potential, every teacher, and every staff member, in the educational institution should be given both training in leadership and the opportunity to expand his or her leadership capabilities. Teachers should be educated about the potential value that enhanced leadership skills of teachers has to:

- the institution
- the students
- the parents
- the community
- the teacher
- assistant teacher
- staff and to every other employee in the school system.

Leadership training and development is no longer for the few, and leadership is no longer by the few. The benefits of leadership were always supposed to be spread among all of us. One benefit of being a leader in an educational institution is that it can bring so much value to so many people so quickly. We declare that there is room for, and the need for, leaders at all levels in every PreK–12 school.

All educators lead. This chapter provides key guidance on how teachers can improve their own leadership capacity regarding how they operate in their schools and in all areas of their lives. The first question we seek to answer is *how* does an educational institution develop the leadership capabilities of its teachers, administrators and staff?

We oppose the common approach that many schools take that all it needs to do is hire some strong leaders. Hiring strong leaders is a necessary, but not sufficient approach to developing the leadership capacities of all of the employees of the schools. Since most schools always have a combination of new teachers, new support staff, inexperienced administrators, and perhaps some veteran teachers who have had no or little leadership development training, merely hiring a handful of effective leaders will always be inadequate to successfully promote a significant leadership capacity initiative for everyone in the school.

A school that invests in and continuously supports leadership development at all levels is most likely to achieve its goals and sustain success. This is not to say that just throwing money at courses or seminars or requiring people to take leadership development courses will by itself guarantee success in every school. It probably will not if those who take the courses are not allowed and encouraged to see the benefit of actually performing leadership roles on a daily basis in their schools.

For a person to even have the desire to be a leader, that person must have a reasonable basis for believing that learning how to be a better leader will produce benefits to their institution and to themselves that are far greater than the costs in time, effort, money, and the inevitable doubt that is often associated with this new endeavor—the learning and work to become a better leader. To support teachers wanting to become better leaders, schools must develop and main a spirit of optimism, inclusion, support, and partnership.

Schools must actively and genuinely create an environment that fuels the reasonable belief that when a teacher becomes a better leader, that the teacher will be able and will be allowed to actually lead and make a bigger difference at the school level. When this occurs, then the money a school or school district spends on leadership development will produce an excellent result and the school will improve to the maximum extent possible through improved leadership by teachers.

Successful leadership development and expansion of leadership opportunities in schools require the right attitude, the right level of delegation and trust, and the right working relationships established by all who work in a school. Frankly, a broad expansion of meaningful leadership opportunities in the school setting, like the one we are prescribing in this book, will often require a change in the culture in schools. No longer will it be appropriate or fitting for a principal to dictate the rules for the school in a top down, hierarchical manner.

Gone will be the days when teachers are expected never to challenge the principal. Command and control leadership, means no leadership opportunities for the many since only a few occupy the command positions and they expect to control everyone else. In such an environment, giving leadership development workshops to those whose role and all of their activities are dictated to them and controlled by the current "leadership of the school," would be the wrong thing to do since it would raise expectations that would never be fulfilled.

The strategies below to expand leadership capacity in educational institutions do not assume that all schools will change overnight to a collaborative form of leadership where those who sit in the top boxes of the organizational chart become great active listeners who motivate every employee by seeking their advice and involvement in helping make key decisions in the schools. However, the strategies below are also not designed just to work at the individual level.

When enough teaches declare or self-identify themselves as leaders, when enough teachers proactively sense and work together with each other and administrators to solve upcoming challenges, when teachers learn that improving their own leadership skills increases student test scores significantly, there will be a groundswell by teachers that will be too strong to resist. Teachers will demand that they not be left out of the leadership development movement that has been sweeping this country for the past decade in so many other sectors, but seems to have bypassed PreK–12 education.

This chapter focuses on leadership at the organizational level, becoming part of the leadership team at your school. This may be a rough and tumble world at first, but over time one will look back at the days when all key decisions in a school were made by a principal or administrators who did not even work in the school, while teachers were ignored, as being "prehistoric." The purpose of this chapter is not to depose the principal.

The purpose is to give the principal the assistance in leading the school that only teachers can provide. It is this leadership assistance that can improve schools significantly, improve the experience of teachers significantly, and improve the reputation of schools in the community.

Teachers become leaders in three stages. First, teachers become better leaders by gaining some leadership skills and confidence that empowers them to think of themselves as a leader (identification). Second, teachers become better leaders by taking on some leadership roles in the school.

Third, and most importantly, teachers become better leaders by demanding to be heard on key issues and by demanding to be included in decision-making that affects their lives and the lives of their students and their parents. By demand, we do not mean performing a sit-in and occupying the principal's office. We mean by negotiating forcefully to get a seat at the table. Getting a seat at the table never means that your position will prevail, but it yields huge benefits on the road to being a leader.

A person becomes a better leader by gaining experience, wisdom and expertise in the decision-making process. If you are at the table, those who are not will feed you information and you will feed them information. This sharing of information will begin to reveal strategies, leverage points in the negotiations, cracks in the other side's position, and will give you strength to pursue your position with greater vigor and energy than one could ever muster not having a seat at the table.

Once a teacher gets a seat at the table, that person will soon know that they belong at the table where the key decisions are made, and it will become second nature for that person to take responsibility at the organizational level to help solve some of the organizational challenges. As a person becomes enrolled, by self-appointment or by selection from those above or below, in the decision-making process, a new level of engagement takes hold and a true leader is born.

As more and more teachers become leaders, the entire school will transform, and more and more teachers, now leaders, will be willing to push hard against the toughest problems. Teachers, in the role of leaders, will not only be engaged at a new level, they will bring their wisdom, experience, insight, and knowledge to every project and every new strategy that is geared to significantly improving and transforming the school.

A teacher begins to become a better leader from the moment the teacher says, "I am now ready to be a leader. I am ready to take responsibility. I am ready to work together to help lead this school, to help improve student performance, to help improve the working conditions of teachers, and to help America improve its PreK–12 educational institutions." This means that teachers must lead themselves, individually and as a group, to constantly look for ways to improve student outcomes and teacher experiences.

Teachers who seek to become better leaders will be willing to be more involved in those areas of decision making and implementation traditionally reserved for principals and the few leaders in top positions of schools. It is legitimate to ask: How are principals and other traditionally recognized and well positioned school leaders going to react to this? We have some answers.

The response will vary widely from principals who will do everything to keep teachers from getting a seat at the decision making table to principals who know that they alone, with their current top team of leaders, cannot improve the school as much as they would like or as much as they could if teachers became better leaders and were given significant leadership development training.

Some principals and top leadership will invite teachers to have a seat at the table, listen attentively, and then ignore every recommendation teachers make. Some will do the right thing and actively work to expand leadership of the school to include teachers and not only give teachers a seat at the decision making table but also give them real implementation authority and delegate to them the responsibility to make new programs work and make old programs work better.

Regardless of how any principal reacts, teachers who seek to become better leaders must be in this for the long haul. Leadership is not what you do on Monday. Leadership is what you do over a span of time—a decade or many decades. The information we provide in this chapter speaks not only to improving the leadership capacity of individual teachers but also to the leadership capacities of everyone in an educational institution and the leadership capacity or leadership density of the educational institution.

Today, in a school setting no one person is a "committee" or sole leader of the school. If schools are going to improve significantly, they will only improve if teachers, trained in leadership, get to participate in the leadership of the school. Teachers who are better leaders will create the environment where they will be accepted over time by the traditional hierarchy of schools as partners in the leadership team at the school, and the school and the students will be better for it.

Previously, we provided a leadership framework that will guide teachers to train themselves to be better leaders, both on an individual, level one, all the way up to level four, the organizational level. This Chapter takes each of the levels we described before and outlines specific actions to promote stronger leadership capacity and stronger leadership *involvement* at each level.

Developing leadership capacity and increasing leadership involvement does not have to occur in some incremental manner or be sequential. In other words, teachers interested in expanding their leadership capacity and increasing their leadership involvement can select actions from each level of leadership. Each teacher can work to help other teachers who want to participate as a leader at every level.

INDIVIDUAL VERSUS ORGANIZATIONAL DEVELOPMENT

One of our co-authors, a school superintendent, recently spoke with a teacher about professional learning communities (PLCs). She was a veteran teacher and one of five members of an elementary PLC, which met once a week in her school. She informed the superintendent that the PLCs were not working well. The teacher complained about how the principal had provided little guidance and coaching.

According to the teacher, the principal had done a poor job of educating the staff in the effective use of PLCs. The principal had also provided very little information about the purpose of PLCs and the rationale for using PLCs. At no time during the conversation did the teacher take any responsibility for the current problems with the PLC, nor did the teacher state what actions the teacher, herself, had undertaken to improve the PLCs.

When asked what had she done to help her own, much less other PLCs, work more effectively, the question that was really being asked was, "What leadership role or responsibility had she taken on to improve the PLCs?" Since the teachers of that school had always looked to the principal for guidance, instruction, and even dictates on just about everything, the teacher's complaints about the principal in that context seemed legitimate.

However, the teacher failed to seize the opportunity created by the lack of principal guidance to create and support the PLCs in the image that the teacher and other teacher leaders could have had for the PLCs. The point of this vignette is that leadership development requires not only spotting a problem but seizing the opportunity at every opening to help address the problem.

A person once said, "When I walk into a room, if I don't see a leader, I lead." This should have been the maxim of the teacher in the PLC situation, but this teacher was always looking for the principal to lead and provide guidance.

The conversation would have been much different if the teacher had said in response to the question, "What leadership role or responsibility had she taken on to improve the PLC's?" "I tried this, and it did not work. I wanted to try this, but I was not allowed to do it. I wanted to get others to work with me to help solve the problem, but I was told, in no uncertain terms, that I did not have the authority to do this and there would be a negative job action against me if I tried to pursue this activity working with others to help improve the PLCs."

All of those are reasonable scenarios in K–12 educational settings and they present a different set of problems than the one we address here. Good leaders do not act as if they re helpless. They know they have a duty to grow as leaders. They demand of themselves that they develop their leadership capacity. They know they have a significant amount of control over whether they reach or get close to their potential as a leader.

When leaders are faced with barriers or obstacles that get in their way of involving themselves in leadership activities, they work long and hard to eliminate the barriers to leadership they face. They may not always succeed, but they take a stand, and they do not give up in the face of recriminations, falling out of favor with those in power, or even negative job actions. They pursue activities until they prevail, or at least get the door opened slightly for others to push into a full open position.

Leaders know that in order to succeed in even getting the door open, they need the skills that studying leadership development can provide. Yet the ultimate goal is not to just get the door opened or just to get a seat at the decision-making table. The goal of leaders who are teachers is to improve PreK–12 education in the United States.

Once a teacher gets a seat at the decision making table, which will take significant leadership skills in itself, the really tough job is to help make and implement decisions that actually improve PreK–12 education in your school and ultimately, in the United States. And that will take even greater leadership skills and capacity than just getting a seat at the table.

Therefore, this chapter outlines additional actions teachers can take to develop excellent, hard core leadership skills. Since there are additional steps schools should take to improve even after teachers become part of the leadership structures of PreK–12 schools, we also venture forth in this chapter to discuss the actions schools should take in the section below.

LEVEL ONE LEADERSHIP

As outlined in Chapter Two, level one leaders know their strengths and areas for growth. These leaders can self-assesses and reflect, can analyze risk and risk tolerance. They continually challenge themselves to deliver better results, to improve and expand their influence. They face the question are they up to the task of getting feedback which can be highly critical, and then doing the really hard work after getting back this feedback on a regular basis and monitoring their individual progress toward achieving their challenging goals

At the school level, there is the parallel question: how many schools are up to the task of helping all teachers have this feedback opportunity and using it to develop level one, two, three, and four leadership capacity among all teachers and staff? How many schools, for example, ask teachers to submit goals at the beginning of the year, and then ignore actively assisting teachers with these goals throughout the year?

How many schools or districts have a culture and rigorous, documented practice, of providing feedback on the quality of every teacher's instruction and on the leadership capacities of their teachers? For all schools that have no such organized and documented feedback mechanisms, individual teachers are faced with three choices. One, create your own feedback system. Two, try to engage the entire school in creating and sustaining this feedback mechanism. Three, complain about it and hope that someone else fixes the problem in your lifetime.

Merely complaining, is actually not an option for a leader. Creating your own feedback system or seeking to have the school create and sustain this feedback system, are viable leadership options. With very little investment, schools can improve both the teachers' and the staff's leadership capacity by helping all of their employees become self-aware with regard to leadership. Individuals can also take steps to ensure they are level one leaders at a minimum. We explore both of these options in depth.

Individual Actions

Level one leadership rests on the premise that one must first understand who he or she is before this leader can lead others successfully and consistently. There are many steps a person can take to become more self-aware. A few are detailed below.

- Compare yourself to the different scales on the four levels of the leadership rubric in Chapter Two. You can do this without involving others. Or take a valid leadership assessment survey instrument which is available from many sources. Then, study the report generated by your answers, which may help you identify strengths and weaknesses. One note—some of your weaknesses may be overdone strengths, so one does not have to be harshly critical of one's self when a weakness is identified.
- Ask and enroll others to help you assess your leadership capacity. Seek feedback. Good leaders understand that their own view of their leadership ability is not the only view that matters. Good leaders might join a critical friends group that meets at least quarterly to assess one another, using a leadership rubric.
- Undertake a "360 degree assessment" of each member of the group of their leadership and other abilities. A "360 degree assessment" is where people in your organization, who are above you, are your equals or peers, and people who are your subordinates, plus yourself, rate you on many attributes of leadership. By seeing how your scores and all other scores given about you compare to each other, there is much to learn about how successful you are as a leader in the eyes of your superiors, your subordinates, and your peers. These assessments are always done

in a confidential manner so that no one can identify any one person who might be rating them.

- Establish for yourself and communicate to others challenging and measurable goals with real timeframes for accomplishing these goals. Every goal has a "by when" date attached to it or is not a real goal, it is merely a hope. Teachers who are trying to become good leaders should establish milestones by which they can track their progress. These goals should challenge the teacher to grow and should inspire the teacher and those around the teacher.
- Develop a leadership growth plan. One should write a specific plan to expand a person's leadership capacity. It might only be a few pages long, and include courses to take, books or articles to read, speeches to hear, leadership responsibilities to take on, and the like.

Organizational Actions

- Schools should seek to create a program that provides all employees the information and support they need to self-assess regularly. Employees should assess themselves on the teacher-evaluation instrument, which should include a section on leadership. If leadership is not a part of the evaluation instrument, employees should assess themselves, using a leadership rubric.
- Schools should provide opportunities for employees to assess strengths and preferences through researched-based instruments. Instruments such as the Myers-Briggs personality inventory, change style indicator, FIRO-B, and others generally provide great insights into a person's talents and preferences. These instruments will not only help raise individuals' awareness of their own abilities they will also help individuals gain insights and perspective (Level Two).
- Schools should seek to help create for all employees and teachers excellent leadership academies. Be sure to provide appropriate incentives for teachers and all employees to participate in these leadership academies. Agenda items might include:
- an understanding of the leadership framework
- personality inventories
- leading without a title
- coaching subordinates and superiors
- having difficult conversations
- understanding and implementing successful change models
- other leadership concepts.
- Build a culture of honest feedback throughout every level of the school. Individuals can attempt to seek feedback on their own, or in small teacher groups that they have generated. However, it would be easier and more

organizationally effective if the entire school or district developed a culture of feedback with scheduled activities so the teachers and staff could plan their activities in a manner that fits in these activities.

LEVEL TWO LEADERSHIP

Many of the actions outlined above will be applicable to help teachers gain perspective, the key element of level two leadership. In addition to the actions identified above, we recommend the following:

Individual Actions

- Become aware of how you often do not listen to or understand fully the perspective of others. Observe others as they either fail or succeed in listening effectively enough to fully understand the reasons for another's position.
- Assess whether you build relationships in order to further communication and if you ask clarifying questions sufficiently to understand the interests of others.
- Review the decision-making activities of yourself and others to see if you or others make decisions based on partial or insufficient information.
- Be willing to suggest to others who are about to make a decision based on incomplete information, that they wait until they get additional information.
- Observe how closely you and others attempt to have close coordination in developing decisions and implementing strategies for success.

Organizational Actions

- Demand that your school have more open meetings to promote dialogue on all key decisions and have the meeting facilitator endeavor to bring out everyone's point of view on key matters.
- Insist that decisions on key issues made in writing or orally include the reasons why the decision came out that way, plus clear statement as to why arguments made against the decision were rejected.
- Suggest the formation of working groups to discuss all key decisions and use those working groups to inform decision-makers of the pros and cons of each potential decision.
- Make sure that your school issues clear statements regarding current policies, not just stating the policies, but stating why these policies were selected over other alternatives.

- Take a stand to argue for your school setting clear organizational standards of excellence that receive a consensus of support from all persons whose actions are to be measured against this standard.
- Work to enroll groups of teachers, and other stakeholders to work together to creatively solve problems. Insist that when such a group deliberates carefully and makes a strong recommendation for a course of action, that the principal of your school and other decision-makers follow their advice when they develop an approach to solve a problem.
- Work to have your school reward continuous learning with significant acknowledgement and recognition programs and not merely small salary increases.

LEVEL THREE LEADERSHIP

Level three leadership focuses on the ability to motivate others successfully to reach their potential. There are numerous activities at the individual level and the organizational level that can increase a person's capacity in this arena.

Individual Actions

- Actively support another teacher or someone else or a group or section of your school, (a class, for example) in an intensive manner in setting a stretch goal and supporting that person or group in achieving it.
- Develop a plan for acknowledging yourself and others for achieving their goals.
- Carefully evaluate individuals' commitment to a project or a goal and help them either keep or restore their full commitment to success of the project or remove them from their key role in the project.
- Include others whose participation you seek and need for success in developing the original plan for the activity.
- Communicate often and clearly all decisions you are making and their rationales so that others can see that you are attempting to be transparent and open with them.
- When you or your school is starting a project or attempting to reach a goal, conduct a stakeholders' analysis and identify each and every group or individual to be affected by the decision, attempt through communication with them to understand their interests and positions, and keep them involved and informed throughout the project.

Organizational Actions

- At your school, take action to insure all stakeholders are included in projects that affect them.
- For all key decisions, demand that your school form decision and advisory committees which include all key stakeholders and all known positions on key areas where a decision will need to be made.
- Insist that your school principal or decision-maker communicate decisions as soon as they are made to all concerned.
- Demand teacher involvement in decision-making and strongly argue for the top leaders of your school to delegate decision-making to the lowest feasible level to allow people to participate in making the decisions that impact their ability to perform their jobs.
- Educate your school of the benefits of promoting reasonable risk-taking by rewarding, or at least not punishing, failures and mistakes, if they occurred as the result of taking a reasonable risk to be innovative and improve the status quo.
- Make sure that your school's human resources department keeps a good and current record of each employee's interests, talents and skills and endeavor to match these interests, talents and skills with key efforts or challenges where there is a good fit.
- Suggest to top decision-makers in the school that they delegate to a person who promotes or comes up with a school improvement idea, the responsibility of building a consensus or garnering support for this school improvement idea before they even get to the planning stage.
- Insist that your school let all teachers and staff know as soon it becomes apparent that changes will need to be made, why changes will need to be made, and let them know clearly how they can participate in making decisions that will guide how or if these, changes will be made.
- Work to instill a culture in your school that promotes adaptability and flexibility as the better responses to new situations rather than developing a culture where rules that were developed to deal with one situation are blindly applied to new situations that were not contemplated when the rule was put into place.
- Create a culture and practice in your school that allows and encourages all teachers and staff in the school to review, and propose changes to policies, procedures and provide real suggestions and solutions to challenges or difficulties faced by the school.
- Make sure that your school encourages and rewards people publicly who identify challenges and problems and who also suggest how to solve the problems.

• Help manage the conversation in the school by discouraging complaints and encouraging persons to make clear requests to change the situation to resolve the matter that is at issue.

LEVEL FOUR LEADERSHIP

Level four includes creating a shared vision and engaging the entire organization to align with and act consistently with that vision.

Individual Actions

• Take a leadership role in a school-wide initiative or class-wide initiative.
• Build a diverse team of people to assist you in accomplishing a big goal of importance to your school.
• Set the highest ethical standards for yourself and do not breach them.
• Form a monthly leadership development support group to help you learn how to accomplish your goals.
• Mentor others on a regular basis to become level four leaders.
• Take good care of yourself and your family, physically, mentally and spiritually.
• Be willing, on a regular basis, to put service above your self-interest.
• Join organizations outside of your school and take leadership roles on major projects with these community-oriented organizations.
• Ensure that the work you do for your school is consistent with your key values and the causes about which you are passionate.
• Create inspiration and enthusiasm from each leadership activities you undertake or encourage others to undertake at your school.
• Make sure that you and others get recognized for your successes.
• Make sure that you quickly acknowledge your mistakes.
• Keep good records, notes, and possibly a diary of your reflections on your leadership efforts, successes, failures, and "takeaways" that represent learning that you will apply in the future.
• Always include diverse groups of people of all experience levels and age levels in the groups you lead and where you participate as a follower.

Organizational Actions

• Insist that your school hold retreats where all persons, with the help of a facilitator, are encouraged to help craft or refine the mission and goals of the school.

- Demand that your school hold open discussions with all teachers and staff about the long-term goals and objectives of the school.
- Make sure that all top leaders of your school encourage discussion among all teachers and staff as to why working with the organization is either fulfilling or not fulfilling, meaningful or not meaningful and address all concerns raised in these discussions.
- Create structures in your school that insure that students are included in a meaningful way as partners in retreats and discussions suggested above.
- Create and obtain consensus, if not unanimous support, for key performance indicators of the school.
- Become key participants in the development and regular updating of a forward-looking strategic plan for your school.
- Make sure all employees pay careful attention to the reputation of your institution and how and why it might be changing.
- Insure that all key activities and strategies of the school are mutually reinforcing and not contradictory by pointing out any contradictory activities, programs, strategies or operational aspects of the school.
- "Deputize" every employee to have the power to report any integrity infraction and enforce all integrity matters in a competent, speedy, and open manner so as to set and enforce the highest standards for integrity throughout the school.

CONCLUSION

These actions at the individual and organizational level represent the starting points where teachers can make significant inroads into the leadership structure and dynamic of your school. They are not exhaustive of what can be done at your school. You will identify other, possibly higher-priority activities that are immediate, even urgent in your school setting. This might deal with:

- student safety
- poor nutrition with the school lunch, or
- poor scheduling which gives students several hours of free time without even a study hall or library where they can study, thus encouraging them to leave campus during the day.

The activities outlined in this chapter are merely illustrative of activities that will help teachers become better leaders. When teachers become better leaders they are not to be pushed into administrative positions. Most teachers want to be teachers, and being a better leader will assist them in being a better teacher and deriving more satisfaction from teaching itself. When teachers pursue these activities cited in this chapter they will become successful in promoting widespread leadership involvement in schools.

Some of these activities will work better and be more feasible for some teachers than for others. When it comes to expanding the leadership capacity at your school, it takes effort, coordination, enrollment, and dealing with and persevering through resistance. It will require a long term commitment on the part of teachers to help promote leadership development and leadership inclusion in your school.

Teachers who participate in strong leadership development efforts at their schools and in their school districts will generate significant future research into this area. They will pave to way as we will learn much in the next decade that will make this process of leadership development among teachers more effective and more efficient as more and more schools adopt a teacher inclusive leadership framework.

As improvements become apparent to teachers, administrators and students alike resulting from leadership development, we expect acceptance of these principles and strategies will increase rapidly. These actions require the investment of time, money, energy, and demand careful planning and meticulous execution. Schools *can* raise the small amounts of funds necessary to start this effort.

Teachers *can* start many of these efforts without any additional funding from the school. As educational outcomes improve as a result of these efforts, and the return on investment becomes clearer and clearer, we anticipate that all stakeholders will endeavor to find and properly allocate the resources necessary to give every teacher significant leadership development training and significant leadership responsibility in the school.

Chapter 4

Leadership as it Applies to Specific Areas in Education

Librarians, Coaches, Special Education Teachers, Counselors, Extracurricular Activity Supervisors, and Students

SPECIAL AREAS OF EDUCATION

This chapter takes a brief look at the unique leadership challenges and leadership approaches for several key domains of PreK–12 education. This section is not designed to summarize all of the work that has been done in leadership in each of these areas. Rather, its goal is to provide key insights about leadership development from each of these key aspects of PreK–12 education.

Each group discussed in this chapter fits well within our broad definition of stakeholders in education, and has a critical and essential role in PreK–12 education. Even more importantly, we believe that sharing some of the leadership ideas from each of these groups with all of the teachers and others who are be reading this book will be of great use to all readers.

LEADERSHIP AND LIBRARIANS

Librarians, for the most part, "get" leadership. Librarians take leadership and management courses to get a master of library science degree. Librarians often seek to improve their leadership skills throughout the course of their careers. The new standards issued by the American Association of School Librarians in 2009 embrace, and even demand, leadership development courses and training for their members and leadership in performing as a school librarian. Since 1998, in virtually every standard, including the latest created by recognized professional associations of librarians, the word *leadership* appears. A few of the standards are listed below.

The National Council for Accreditation of Teacher Education (NCATE) has standards for librarians and guidelines for preparing candidates for library media professionals for service and leadership. The American Association of School Librarians and the Association for Educational Communications and Technology in 1998 declared a pivotal role for the school library media professional in "leadership."

In fact, one standard for the profession requires a librarian to take a "leadership role in developing district/school library resource selection." Since 1998 virtually all schools that provide degrees in library science teach leadership skills as a required component of the course work necessary to secure a degree. Since 1998 the standards and causes on leadership for librarians have envolved.

Wherever you look, in the training of librarians, in their daily work, or in their views regarding their own jobs, you see strong evidence of three key elements:

- The field of library science has determined that strong leadership skills are an essential part of being a successful librarian.
- Librarians often think of themselves as leaders and undertake courses of study to improve their leadership skills.
- The leadership skills of a librarian represent a significant attribute that contributes to their success.

There are several straightforward reasons why librarians must learn leadership skills to perform their job well.

- Librarians are called upon every day to lead students in the process of learning.
- Librarians often take the lead to collaborate with teachers to develop learning programs.
- Research shows that next to the school principal, the school librarian has the most complete knowledge of the school's organization and curriculum and librarian leadership benefits the entire school.
- Librarians run a school department because they manage significant budgets and physical space and run learning resources.
- Librarians have to manage a myriad of relationships in a school.
- Librarians have a direct relationship with administrative personnel and must negotiate regarding many aspects of the areas where they manage.

Upon a careful reading of these five job elements, we actually find more similarities in these job elements with the job elements of teachers than we find differences. We acknowledge that in some respects the role of a teacher and the role of a librarian are different. However, in so many critical aspects, especially as they relate to students, their roles have many similarities and librarians view themselves often as teachers.

It is insightful that librarians and the professional associations that set their standards, set the degree requirements, and foster improvement in the field of library science have placed such a high, and center stage, emphasis on leadership. Leadership plays a central role in the training, in the identity, in the day to day job related activities of librarians. It certainly appears that associations and organizations that seek to improve teaching in the United States could learn from the strides in leadership development made by the field of library science in the past decade.

The professional standards emphasizing leadership for librarians are straightforward and on the mark. They have evolved significantly since 1998 to continue to emphasize leadership as a key building block in the profession of librarians. We find it instructive as a key goal of improving the leadership attributes and skills of librarians is to improve the student outcomes of those students who come in contact with librarians.

Students have benefitted greatly from librarians embracing leadership development as a core competency of their profession. We encourage teachers to check with librarians and their professional associations, including the American Association of School Librarians www.ala.org, about the leadership courses available for librarians and the research that shows how library leadership helps schools and students. We encourage associations that represent teachers to learn about the most useful leadership approaches that are being taught to librarians.

We find it very instructive regarding leadership development that there exists a great example right in the school setting of how librarians, individually, as a whole, and as a profession, have benefitted and continue to benefit greatly from such a strong emphasis on of leadership development as a core skill of the profession. Current research on leadership and librarians can be found at www.lrs.org, the Library Reference Service.

Just as Karen Huffman, senior applications and database administrator, information systems and technology, with National Geographic recently stated, she is actively thinking about planning an activity in southern Maryland that can help bridge the divide she sees between librarians and teachers. If a divide does exist between teachers and librarians, it is our hope that through leadership development courses where teachers and librarians, along with coaches and physical education teachers, all get to participate together, that some of this divide might be reduced and the leadership lessons learned can be shared with all who work in our schools.

LEADERSHIP AND COACHES

Coaches rarely receive any formal leadership training. However, there is no question that leadership is a critical element of their job. In fact, coaches of competitive athletes, especially at the high school level, are actually responsible for the behavior of their players twenty-four hours a day. To prove this point, if a coach of a successful baseball, soccer, basketball, football, golf, tennis, or any other sport has many members of the team go off and do something against the law such as underage drinking, theft, fights, etc., on a regular basis and gets caught, that coach will soon be fired.

Coaches know they are role models and seek to live by the rules of life they teach their players. The tell their players that they will not remembered for that pass, shot, or hit, but they will be remembered by their fellow players and fellow students by how they treated them. Coaches are not always successful, but they always try to teach their players such key leadership values as:

- persistence
- playing by the rules
- helping the other person
- honor/sportsmanship
- respect
- living a healthy lifestyle
- the value of effort and hard work
- a healthy competitive spirit
- creating a lasting legacy by what you do in all aspects of your life

Coaches know that their job is not just to teach skills associated with their sport, but to instill a sense of passion, a sense of mission, and a sense of importance not only to the sport but also to everything the student does in relation to that sport. Coaches insist on encouraging students to:

- live up to their potential
- give credit to others
- work harmoniously in a team environment
- foster courage
- defeat fear

Coaches teach the essence of leadership to their players. A coach's insistence on constant improvement, the art of practice, the importance of always being on time, and the importance of being fully prepared for every foreseeable challenge that the athlete can face are central tenets of a coach's teachings for students.

Coaches have to generate excellence in their athletes, and they know the value of quick, positive reinforcement when a student does something right. Coaches treat each student as an individual although much of their time they coach many students at once. They know a certain level of effort by one student athlete will improve their performance, while demanding that same level of effort from another student, who may be injured, could cause that student great harm.

Coaches are trained to provide physical education and the knowledge of sports. In the category of coaches, we include all physical education teachers. We understand that schools have cut back on physical education programs since the time when the three authors of this book were required to take one hour of physical education almost every day of their PreK–12 experience.

These cutbacks put even more pressure on coaches and physical education teachers to make the most out of every minute they spend with students. Coaches know that two days before an important game, the practice must be done well, and if practice is missed by a student or not well managed by the coach, this hour, just two days before a big game, cannot be "made up" at some later date.

Coaches often say that their job is to "get to the heart" of the student and to infuse in that student the confidence to try things of a physical nature that are difficult and challenging. Further, all coaches and physical education teachers know that they are putting their students into a competitive environment and that every student does not take well to such direct physical competitive challenges.

Coaches are nurturers, but they know how to be demanding of themselves and of their students. During our interviews with coaches, we heard them say, "Coaches should be more like teachers, and teachers should be more like coaches." We do believe that as teachers and coaches seek to become better leaders, there is much that teachers and coaches can learn together and from each other in the leadership development arena.

We applaud coaches for their strong leadership roles and how far they have come in the field of leadership development when they are given precious few tools or leadership development courses by their employers, our schools. We encourage schools and school districts to recognize the vast benefits that providing coaches and physical education teachers with leadership development courses and instruction could provide.

Knowing coaches and physical education teachers as we do, we are assured that whatever leadership skills and attributes coaches and physical education teachers learn from future leadership courses offered to them, they will pass on to their students. When teachers and coaches become better leaders, we can be assured that students will become better leaders as well.

SPECIAL EDUCATION TEACHERS AND
TEACHERS OF SPECIAL NEEDS STUDENTS

The leadership challenges of special education teachers and teachers of special needs students are enormous. The authors have sat in sessions where individualized education plans have been discussed, often in very contentious environments. We have had the benefit of special education teachers teaching our siblings and the sons and daughters of our closest friends. We know the difficult circumstances in which special education teachers operate in our new environment of "mass customization" of educational plans for students, and the increase in students diagnosed with autism and other special needs.

The *Journal of Special Education Leadership* is published by the Council of Special Education Administrators (CASE), a division of the Council for Exceptional Children, a leading association in the special needs educational arena. However, in the Center for Exceptional Children's 18 practice areas, leadership does not show up as a practice area. The College of Teacher Education and Leadership at Arizona State University, has a master's in special education, plus has a bachelor of arts degree in "Early Childhood Education and Leadership."

A brief review of the literature and publications that discuss leadership in the special education arena shows that this literature is directed primarily to administrators and not to teachers. The teachers who are special education teachers could benefit from many of the leadership skills taught in this book and available in leadership development courses. Special education teachers must be able to form successful relationships with parents, administrators, and must be able to form and lead teams that come together for individual educational programs.

Special education teachers must have strong advocacy skills, excellent problem-solving skills, superior communication skills, well-developed listening skills, and must be able to manage some of the most challenging educational areas for programming that exist in the school building. Special education teachers know that for some special education children and their parents, it is the teacher to whom the parents and even the child look to for leadership. Some children from all sectors of society in America do not have parents or even one parent who is in tune with the education their child is receiving.

However, many children, including many special education children do have parents or one parent who would like to be better informed about their children's education. Further, these parents would like to be more involved in helping their child or children learn more effectively. It is the role of the special education teacher, as overburdened and overworked as he or she may be, to be able to leverage and lead those willing and interested parents and help those parents become more effective educators of their own children. Enrollment of this type is a classic leadership attribute and skill. Great leadership skills are needed to be an effective enroller, but great leaders are those who, as President Reagan stated, are able to bring out the best in others.

Bringing out the best in parents to assist their children, both special needs and non–special needs children, is a leadership best practice for teachers. We understand the huge challenges teachers face in enrolling some parents in being an active educational partner with the teacher to teach the child. We know the time demands can be great to undertake the effort of helping parents educate their special needs children more effectively, but leaders know how to get things done quickly.

We urge those associations that work with special needs educators to put leadership on the list of "practice" or professional development areas. Additional leadership skills and behaviors of special needs teachers can pay huge dividends for the student, the parent or parents, and for the special education teacher.

SUPERVISORS OF EXTRACURRICULAR ACTIVITIES

Many teachers are involved in supervising extracurricular activities including:

- Student council
- Yearbook
- Bake sales and talent shows
- Band
- Sports teams
- Carnivals
- Math, language clubs
- Debate team
- Field trips
- Rotaract, key, and other service clubs
- Cheerleading
- Hundreds of other extracurricular clubs and activities

These activities are so important for the growth and entertainment of students in the PreK–12 arena. In these areas, teachers are always acting as true leaders. Teachers help organize the students, the events, and the programs for the school year. Teachers gather and secure resources from parents, businesses, and find creative ways to finance these extracurricular activities. Teachers delegate activities to students at every opportunity. Teachers evaluate the programs, always looking to improve the programs and increase the number of participants each year.

Teachers can put the leadership development lessons of this book into practice when they organize and supervise extracurricular activities. Extracurricular activities can be viewed by teachers as a key practice area for practicing their leadership skills. These activities can become a valued path for teachers as they want to become better leaders. The size, budget, or growth of an extracurricular activity is not the key measure of how big a leadership test the extracurricular activity is for the teacher.

It is the quality of the program and the impact the program has on the students. This is the area where teachers can teach students how to become better leaders. Every extracurricular activity requires leadership not just to expand, or become the best yearbook possible or a winning math club, but to survive year in and year out. Most importantly, the goal of every teacher leading extracurricular activities should be to maximize the benefit to the students who participate, and to the school as well.

Maximizing the benefits of an extracurricular activity is a constant endeavor for the excellent or aspiring leader. In this environment, the teacher-leader should seek feedback not only from other teachers and parents about program, but also from students. The teacher who seeks to become a better leader will take this feedback from the students and all other sources and develop a plan to make the extracurricular activity more beneficial to the students.

Leaders look to all available resources for every project they lead or co-lead. They bring these resources together, organize them, and deploy them to improve the project. In many extracurricular activities, the number one resource the teacher has is the students themselves. Students are a great resource in schools, and for teachers who are seeking to become better leaders, the better a teacher understands and experiences students as resources, the better the leader a teacher can be.

Many schools have students participate as mentors to other students. Many schools have students involved in the leadership of extracurricular activities. Many schools have their students, as a requirement of graduation from high school, volunteer a certain number of hours in the community. All of these activities attest to the significant resource students are in PreK–12 schools. In Washington, D.C., in the mid 1990s, students as young as 5th graders, were expected to volunteer in the community on a regular basis.

Viewing students as a key PreK–12 resource, in ways described below in the section on students, is a small expansion of how teachers lead students to take leadership roles and responsibilities in student organizations and student extracurricular activities. Not every student will rise successfully to the occasion of being a leader of an organization or extracurricular activity, but it is a great training ground for both teachers and students to practice and develop their leadership skills.

STUDENTS

No book on how leadership by teachers can significantly improve schools would be complete without a section devoted to students. Yet, in the literature on leadership in education, students are rarely even mentioned. Teachers lead students in their classroom. No one can argue with this proposition. Teachers set the agenda, handle discipline issues, obtain the behavior they seek from students (most of the time), and guide students through a rigorous learning process that results in significant student achievement.

An important question typical of the questions that leaders ask themselves all the time is: "Is there anything else for teachers to do when it comes to leading students?" And, "Is there anything students, if they were better led by teachers, could do to help teachers be better leaders?" The answer to both of these very important questions is "Yes."

Teachers have always served as leaders of their students. Sometimes teachers have shined and performed exemplary leadership and shown a student that a student had a particular gift, talent, or ability in a certain area, and led them to explore a career in this area. In other cases, teachers have been able to lead a student by carefully showing a student that he or she is consistently making a mistake or not learning an area because of a failure in the student's approach.

Some teachers have been able to show struggling students how to learn in a certain way that eliminates the student feeling that the student is incapable of learning. Teachers, acting as leaders, have helped students realize how smart they are. Teachers exercising strong leadership skills set standards for their students, show students their full potential, and enroll and encourage students to be as good a student, and as good of a person, as that student can be.

When teachers lead their students, they generate enthusiasm by the student in the learning process. Almost every teacher would rather spend an hour helping a struggling student than spending that hour on themselves, either going to the gym or reading a great novel or just relaxing. Teachers lead students when they help students find and explore subject matters of great interest to the particular student, thereby promoting the interest of the student in that area.

One of the authors had a daughter who was quite adept at doing fractions in the first grade even though fractions had not yet been taught in the school curriculum. As students are prone to do, the student starting showing other students how to do fractions in the first grade math class without the teacher noticing it at first. But soon, the teacher caught on to what was going on in the class and not only told the student she could not do this but contacted the parents to tell them that their daughter was misbehaving in class by teaching her fellow classmates fractions and it had to stop.

The parents informed the teacher that their daughter would not be instructed by her parents to stop teaching other students about fractions in math class because their daughter said that all of the students she was teaching loved fractions, got them "right away," and by doing this students were happier to be in math class than they were before. The parents then asked the teacher if the teacher could teach fractions as part of the math curriculum.

The teacher began to teach fractions. The students in this first grade class learned not only fractions but also that they could learn math at a pretty high level. Teachers are promoters of learning and as teachers become better leaders, as this teacher became a better leader through experimenting with fractions for first graders, teachers will become better promoters of student learning.

At first, the teacher saw the student who was teaching her fellow students as a "problem." Soon, however, she saw this student as a "resource" and allowed her students' interest in fractions to influence her curriculum choice for a short period of time thus becoming a better leader. In the students' eyes, the teacher became a better teacher as well.

Leaders listen to their followers and seek feedback from their followers. The example of the first grade student teaching fractions to her fellow students shows us two things. First, it shows us that even at the first grade level, figuring out what interests students and supporting those interests when they are consistent with the goals of PreK–12 education, can help make a teacher a better leader. Second, it shows that the teacher-student relationship can never be merely a one-way communication. It must be an interaction.

By listening carefully to students' desires as to what they want to learn, teachers can craft educational programs that inspire students. As will be discussed below in the chapter on leadership theory, the leader-follower relationship should be viewed as a partnership. This is called the leader-member exchange theory of leadership. This theory also states that the ability of the leader to lead is always a function of the support the leader has from followers.

Leaders seek support from their followers on a constant basis and seek to learn from their followers. This basic notion has important practical applications for leadership for teachers. It should never be the goal of a teacher just to be liked by all of the students. However, it should be the goal of every teacher to have every student respect the teacher and respect the institution of the school and the enormous effort that we go through in American to educate our youth.

Teachers should actively undertake activities that effectively garner the support, even the enthusiastic support, of their students. One way of doing this, we have discussed, is to notice where every student's major areas of interest lie and take the extra step of helping that student promote learning in that area of interest whenever that area of interest is consistent with the objectives of the school, broadly defined. This act of leadership will assist that student become a better learner and become more enthusiastic about learning.

Leaders want to receive feedback so they can improve. During the school day, teachers spend more of their time with students that with any other group in the school building. Teachers evaluate students every day and the reason why teachers give grades to students is to give them a strong incentive to do well, and to identify areas where they are not doing well so corrective action can take place. The same theory and rationale holds true for why students, beginning at some grade level in PreK–12, should regularly evaluate their teachers.

Certainly, the types of evaluation tools and questions asked will be different in order to gain the best information from students at different grade levels. While some teachers may oppose this for fear of what students might say about them, there are many ways to structure evaluations so that it encourages students to provide honest, constructive feedback to teachers who could benefit from this feedback in becoming not only better teachers but also better leaders.

The issue of student evaluations of teachers in the PreK–12 setting, we admit, can have people of goodwill take different positions on this issue. Certainly, if a teacher wants to have his or her students evaluate the teacher, there should never be a road block put in front of the teacher by the administration. If teachers in the early efforts of such evaluations want to be assured that these evaluations will not be a critical factor in their being retained or reassigned, this concern can be accommodated.

Over time, these evaluations by students will, we believe, yield data and information that will be very helpful for those teachers who want to become better teachers and for those teachers who want to become better leaders. The larger issue is not whether students should evaluate teachers. The larger issue is for teachers, as they become better leaders, to look for an entire range of ways they can engage students:

- as partners
- by encouraging students to make suggestions regarding how to improve the school
- by seeking input from students regarding how to improve their teaching

As the authors asked student after student in the PreK–12 school system, "How could students help improve the school?", it became abundantly clear that those students we asked had never been asked this question before. Leaders know that they can gain valuable information from places that others may not even consider to look.

In the fable, it was the child who spoke the truth that the emperor had no clothes. If the truth had been that the emperor wore beautiful clothes that day, it probably would have been a child who first stated how beautiful the emperor's clothes were. As teachers become better leaders, those teachers who treat their students as partners (consistent with the leader-member exchange theory of leadership discussed below) will consistently find that many, if not most, of their students can be very valuable resources to the schools. Listening to students and actively seeking their input can improve the educational process and can contribute significantly to improving student outcomes in schools.

Students can assist teachers to become better leaders, but only when teachers view students as having the capability of assisting effectively in that role. Students can help teachers improve their teaching skills by giving them honest, regular feedback or evaluations. Students, before they can ever really help improve our school system, must be asked by teachers the question, "What suggestions do you have for improving our school?"

Students, in some situations, will be so shocked by that question the first, second, and even third time they are asked, that they may not have great answers. However, over time, as teachers who want to be better leaders continue to ask students this question and continue to encourage students to ask each other this question, and form groups to discuss this question and report out their recommendations for improving their schools, their responses to this all-important question will mature over time and will assist teachers in becoming better leaders.

Our suggestions for having students help improve schools and help teachers become better leaders is just one of potentially hundreds of approaches that can be employed to bring students up to the level of being able to provide input into the improvement of schools and the improvement of leadership skills of teachers. One of the authors of this book, while in high school, was asked by the teacher who was responsible for student council if he would help the school integrate its extracurricular activities while the school was working through school desegregation.

Here is a great example of a student, who had been very outspoken in favor of integration when it was very unpopular in his home town in the 1960s, being asked to work in an area where he obviously cared deeply, had been outspoken, and felt he could contribute to helping integration working in his high school. This student saw the huge challenges that the school faced and helped bring along other students in the school not to oppose integration as it was being court ordered.

Viewing students as a resource is nothing new. Leaders take what is not new and bring it up a notch or two to a new level. Not every effort to lead students into a better partnership with teachers (and school administrators) will work out. However, the act of starting to engage students and viewing them as a potential resource that could help improve the schools, is a true act of leadership on the part of the school.

Viewing parents of students in the same way, as people who can assist the schools improve, has been done in virtually every PreK–12 school. Teachers who want to become better leaders can also focus on working more successfully to create partnerships with parents to help lead them to be more supportive and participative in the education of their children and in the improvement of the schools. Schools throughout the country have administration-led efforts to encourage businesses to donate resources, provide guest teachers, and support the schools. Teachers often participate in this.

Teachers, acting as leaders, could become even more involved in calling on businesses to donate items to schools, to provide guest teachers on certain topics, to help manage extracurricular activities, and could ask businesses to help in other ways to make our schools a better place for our students and our teachers. Leaders seek out help when challenges are greater than their ability to solve them.

The challenges we face today are greater than any one teacher, one principal, one school district superintendent, one state or federal Secretary of Education, or any one of us can solve. When an opportunity is as great as the opportunity to improve our schools, improving the leadership ability of our teachers can produce special benefits for our schools and our teachers.

CONCLUSION

This chapter of the book calls on all segments of the school—administrators, teachers, librarians, coaches, special education teachers, staff and teachers' assistants, students, and parents—to be viewed as key resources that can be tapped to help improve our schools. Leaders seek resources in an inclusive manner. Leaders find solutions to challenges that actually bring people closer to them rather than drive them further away. Inclusion is a key word for twenty-first century leaders, and this chapter has attempted to show how to include all personnel in schools, including students, in helping improve our schools.

We may not all agree on the best approaches to have teachers become better leaders. We may not agree on the best roles students can play in helping schools improve and helping teachers become better leaders. But we must all agree that in order to improve schools, we need to leverage more and better resources than we have in the past. School budgets will not grow dramatically in an economy as challenged as ours.

However, with the great talent of teachers, students, and those in the community who want to improve our schools, we can all agree that if teachers could become better leaders, they could be more effective at securing and leverage key resources that will benefit the schools of our nation. We can also all agree that improving our schools and improving student outcomes are some of the most important goals of our nation.

Chapter Five will give you two critical tools for becoming a better leader: 1) a clear understanding of leadership theory, and 2) a better understanding of the true underpinnings of motivation. Chapter Five includes leadership best practices and key approaches to keeping others and yourself motivated and on track to becoming a better leader in the school environment.

Chapter 5

Leadership Theory and Practice

LEADERSHIP THEORY

Leadership is what teachers and most people in education do day in and day out. They lead students. Knowing the ten generally accepted theories of leadership, and the theories regarding motivation and many of the brands of leadership, can be helpful as teachers seek to become better leaders. This chapter provides an overview of leadership theory and practice and is designed to be a reference guide for the reader. In Appendix B to this book, we have provided a description of approximately 90 brands of leadership currently found in the leadership literature today.

TEN LEADERSHIP THEORIES

There are ten specific theories of leadership. However, there is no general unifying theory of leadership which has been described previously in the leadership literature. Each of these theories tries to explain how leaders become leaders or how leaders work when they are leading people. The first nine theories are based on Northouse's work and are presented in an "evolutionary" order. Each theory builds on the previous theory. The tenth theory is a contribution to the leadership literature by one of the authors of this book and dates back to the Jethro/Moses story in the Book of Exodus. The ten theories are as follows:

1. **The Trait Theory:** People with certain favorable physical, mental, personality, and emotional traits are more likely, if not destined, to be leaders.

89

2. **The Style Approach:** Leadership is a function of the style of behavior a person brings to a situation. Three typical styles of leadership activity include:

   - delegating authority to others as one delegates responsibility
   - demanding that others follow a very strict interpretation of the rules the leader lays out for them allowing little creativity or spontaneity
   - letting others set the rules as they seek to implement activities

3. **The Situational Approach:** Leaders must "read" a situation accurately and determine what combination of supportive and directive behaviors is appropriate to achieve the goal of the leader. This leadership theory suggests that leaders adapt their styles and behavior based on understanding the full content and context of the situation in which they are operating, their role, the goals of the situation, and the resources they have to use and direct.

4. **The Contingency Theory:** Understanding and developing successful leadership behaviors is based on analyzing three key factors: leader-member relations, task structure, and position power. Contingency theory shows how the success of certain styles of leadership is contingent on the circumstances in which they are used. Thus, this theory suggests that the relationship between the leaders and the followers should have a strong impact on the leader and the appropriate leadership style that will be effective in that situation.

5. **Path-Goal Theory:** This is the motivational theory of leadership. This theory suggests that a major goal of leadership is to stimulate performance and satisfaction among those led by the leader. Under this theory the classic behaviors of the leader are:

   (1) to identify goals and to secure "buy in," support, enthusiasm, ownership of these goals by followers
   (2) to identify all key obstacles and barriers to achieving the goals
   (3) ensure proper training and resources for followers in their effort to achieve goals
   (4) to organize and direct the actions of the followers in their efforts to achieve goals
   (5) to monitor all activity and guide any changes in strategy, resources, and actions necessary to achieve goals
   (6) to identify precisely and accurately when the goal is achieved or the shortcomings that result from the effort
   (7) to acknowledge and reward systematically all followers for contributions in the effort to achieve the goals
   (8) to set new goals and expectations for the group and repeat the process

6. **Leader-Member Exchange Theory:** This theory has been previously mentioned in this book as it relates to the relationship between teachers, acting as leaders, as students. This theory posits that leadership is a function of a relationship in which followers give to a leader leadership status and responsibilities and leaders accept that status and perform leadership acts that the followers accept. The relationship between the leader and followers is one of partnership rather than control. Power is shared by followers or members with the leader, and the leader's ability and authority to lead is always a function of the support he or she has from the members or followers.

7. **Transformational Leadership:** Leadership is a process where leaders and followers work together in a manner that changes and transforms individuals and groups. It is a dynamic process that assesses the followers' needs and motives and seeks the input of the followers at each critical stage in the leadership process. Transformational leadership presupposes that the goal of the leader is to promote change and improvement for the betterment and with the assistance of the followers. This type of leadership has an explicit goal of turning followers into future leaders.

8. **Team Leadership:** This theory assumes that all leaders are leaders of teams and the major functions of a leader are:
   (1) to help the group determine which goals and tasks it wants to achieve
   (2) to help create enabling processes and direct the group so that it achieves the goals and tasks
   (3) to keep the group (and the leader) supplied with the right resources, training, and supplies
   (4) to set standards for behavior, success, and ethics
   (5) to diagnose and remedy group deficiencies
   (6) to forecast impending environmental changes to help inform and steer the group appropriately
   (7) to help maintain and defend the group by organizing it and ensuring its proper internal functioning

9. **Psychodynamic Approach:** Leadership requires that leaders understand their own psychological makeup and the psychological makeup of those they lead. Leaders using this theory are those who understand:
   (1) the followers' attitudes, potential, behaviors, and expected responses to leadership
   (2) the level of maturity of followers and its impact on their responses to leadership actions
   (3) the desires and motivational keys of followers

(4) the meaning and interpretation by followers of language, behavior, symbols, and situations

(5) the proper balance of dependence and independence appropriate for a given group of followers

(6) the proper psychological relationship between the leader and followers

(7) of the psychodynamic interplay between the leader and followers and between and among leaders as well

10. Leaders of Leaders: This theory suggests that the job of a leader of followers is completely different from that of a leader of leaders. Leaders of followers are mainly "problem solvers." Leaders of leaders establish platforms and seek to create an environment so that followers can act as leaders themselves, solve their own "problems," and make excellent decisions consistent with the platform that the leader of leaders sets.

In addition, the leaders of leaders concept incorporates the idea that the platform set by the leader of leaders will improve over time because the followers and other leaders will be encouraged to test the platform in the real world, find deficiencies, and report proposed improvements for the platform to the leader of leaders. The major role of the leader of leaders is to create this platform and not to make decisions in particular situations. This job is delegated to the leaders whom the leader of leaders leads.

Each of these theories is relevant to teachers who intend to become better leaders. This review of leadership theory shows that there are many parts to leadership. It also shows that learning leadership theory and applying it in the daily practice of teaching is something that each and every teacher can do. These theories of leadership can be easily learned and applied. They are both practical and serve as a general guide regarding how teachers can think about understanding leadership more fully. Below, we identify ten leadership principles that serve as a guide to teachers.

TEN LEADERSHIP PRINCIPLES

Ten key leadership principles are relevant to helping teachers become better leaders in the classroom, in the school, in their lives and in the eyes of their students are:

1) ***Work on Philosophy First.*** *Philosophy* means your beliefs, goals, and priorities. Developing your own philosophy will make your leadership efforts consistent and, in addition, will make it easier for others to

understand "where you are coming from." The philosophy of teachers is almost always very well-developed by the time the teacher becomes a teacher. When leaders lead, they need to not only know their own philosophy but also understand the philosophy of others.

This requires taking the time to listen to stakeholders and discuss with them at the outset any differences they have with you regarding philosophy. When leaders can help groups agree on philosophy they go a long way toward creating the unity and team approach that can help everyone achieve a goal or overcome a challenge.

2) ***Focus.*** Leaders must set priorities. Multitasking does not mean that we can actually do two things at once. It only means that in a nanosecond we can switch from doing one thing to doing another thing and then go back to what we were doing before. The most critical resource of the leader is the leader. If the leader gets stretched too thin and works on too many activities, they will lead poorly, if at all. Setting priorities means figuring out not only what should be done first but also which projects and activities get more resources and more preparation, and which get less.

Setting priorities also requires being able to anticipate what could happen in the future. Sometimes, because we did not anticipate the future very well, what has become urgent is not even that important. But, because we did not anticipate it, it must be dealt with immediately and gets in the way of items that have much longer-term importance. The more one is able to focus, the fewer distractions one will have. Distractions not only drain energy they stifle our ability to be leaders.

3) ***Be Confident.*** Leaders cannot and should not always be confident in their ultimate success on any project or achieving any goal. However, leaders must be confident that they are on the right path, that the objective is worthy, that achieving a goal will improve the situation, and most importantly, must be confident that they have the right capabilities either to help lead or to participate in a useful way toward achieving success.

Confidence means believing in your current abilities and your ability to improve your abilities. Overconfidence means believing your abilities are greater than they are. Underconfidence means believing your capabilities are less than they are. As Henry Ford once said, "Whether you believe you can accomplishing something or not, either way you are right." Confidence is contagious and represents a clear reading of your capabilities and your ability to improve. Almost every leader is a better leader after completing even the smallest project where leadership skills are deployed.

The best way to boost confidence of any person who wants to be a better leader is for that person to take on a project and serve in the role of leader. Some projects only take one or two people and can last only a week, require little or no money, and can provide both great lessons and the building blocks for improved leadership confidence when they are undertaken and when they are completed.

4) ***Develop a Picture of What Success Looks Like***. Goals can be and are often expressed in numbers. However, the process of achieving these goals and how success will really look is best visualized at the beginning of any endeavor. A leader's ability to get others to see the same image of success is often very valuable in getting people to work together successfully. Visualizing success is also a key component to be able to communicate the goal without using notes, without being nervous in speaking to a group, and in successfully leading others to realize the full benefits of achieving the goal.

5) ***Be Systemic.*** Leaders accomplish as much as they need to accomplish and keep track of all of the things that are going on because they develop and employ systems that help them do this. For example, having a team you lead issue a report at a certain time each week allows you to avoid asking "When will that report be done?"

   Project management systems can be as simple as making sure you have all of the necessary contact information from everyone in a meeting before anyone leaves the meeting or be as complicated as tracking five, ten or even a hundred teams all working on different aspects of the same project. Whenever a leader finds that he or she is doing something that is repeatable or a project has many repeatable steps, developing a system to deal with and guide the performance of these tasks saves time and improves performance in the long run. Modern computer systems make this much easier than ever before.

6) ***Secure Resources for Any Activity You Will Lead as Early in the Process as Possible.*** Whether it is time that you reserve on your calendar for an activity, money you need for supplies for your classroom, a space for a group to meet, or team members to assist you with a project or activity, the farther out in time you really need these resources, the easier it is for you to secure them.

   How often has your energy or the energy been drained by a person when they don't have the resources they need to do something in the next day or two? Resource planning, resource acquisition, resource deployment, and resource accountability and documentation are all equally important/ Not one of these key elements of leadership can be done well in a hurry or at the last minute. Every leader should know how to develop a simple budget for an activity that is accurate, that provides enough resources to deal with some unforeseen challenges, and educates all participants in the activity how money will be spent to achieve the goal.

7) ***Operationalize Key Concepts and Goals.*** Every opportunity can only be achieved through concrete action. Future action must be guided by feedback from present and recent action. Leading projects is somewhat like leading a dance with a partner. It is not enough to know the right steps. You must know the right order for the steps as well. It is not always easy to know what order is best for performing actions that will lead most effectively and most efficiently toward achieving the goal or fulfilling the opportunity.

   Setting the schedule of activities, often with significant input from others, is often a critical task of leaders. If a leader thinks it will take five years to achieve a goal, it is important to have a schedule that covers this five year period. Obviously, such a schedule will be much more detailed and intense in the first weeks and months of the project than in the fourth and fifth years. However, leaders must try to keep activities on schedule and must set realistic schedules to achieve a goal or risk losing the enthusiasm of not only their followers but also of themselves.

8) ***Inspire and Motivate.*** Leaders inspire themselves, motivate themselves, and then inspire and motivate others. An important role of a leader is to acknowledge each person's work on any project or activity. This acknowledgement must be done in a manner that is meaningful to them and to their community.

9) ***Hold People Accountable and Secure High Levels of Productivity, Morale, and Goodwill.*** Leaders need to take action when someone repeatedly says they are going to do something, and they fail to do it. They need to replace ineffective people on their team or redeploy them to a part of the project where they can be more successful.

   Productivity is not only a function of good morale. It is a function of having clear roles and clear goals, and being managed well. High morale is essential and leaders should know when it is dipping and why, and take effective action to improve it. Goodwill is so important to leaders that an entire book could be written about it. Every project does better if there is goodwill among all of the participants.

Education improves if there is goodwill between teachers and students, teachers and administrators, parents, taxpayers, and the general community. There are times when goodwill is impossible to achieve. However, leaders must endeavor to achieve goodwill, avoid longstanding grudges whenever possible, and to attempt to work together with goodwill whenever possible.

10) ***Build Leadership Density.*** Leaders should welcome the opportunity of helping others become better leaders. While it is not true all the time that the more leaders the better on a given project or effort to achieve a goal, when a leader can distribute leadership on projects to others, the project can benefit from gaining different perspectives, having people participate where they are most effective, and encouraging others to bring in other people to the project.

The opposite of building leadership density is micromanagement or being a control "freak." These are among the worst mistakes a leader can make. Leadership training, mentoring, constructive feedback, encouraging self-reflection are all steps towards promoting improving the leadership density on any project or in any organization. One of the goals of this book is to increase the leadership density among teachers in the United States.

When there is more leadership density, many people on a project are encouraged and empowered to take initiative, to solve their own challenges, to come up with their own solutions, and to teach others proudly what they have accomplished. Two of the strongest forces that prevent the development of leadership density are fear and insecurity. Fear is often created by leaders who do not want others to become better leaders. Insecurity, or self-doubt, is often created by people who do not want to take any risk because of their concern that they might fail and that failure will have very negative consequences for them.

Leaders fail very often, but they pick themselves up and try again. Leaders should always challenge other leaders that seek to create fear in any organization, especially schools. Leaders should also seek to help people get over their insecurities by giving them assignments where they feel confident enough to take risks, where they know they can pick themselves up after a mistake or failure, and where they can build confidence over time.

These theories and principles of leadership are guideposts to teachers who want to become better leaders. For some, thinking of leadership as a means to solving problems, is also a good approach to finding ways to become a better leader. One basic notion of leadership defines it as 'problem solving.'

Leaders are people who solve problems and often people who see problems and understand them first.

This simplified notion of leadership, problem solving, describes much of what leaders do. Leaders must spot or identify problems early enough so that a solution that is not too costly can solve the problem. Although leadership will always be about solving problems, there is a new branch of leadership that is not just about solving problems.

Rather than leadership just solving problems, many view leadership as about seeing and fulfilling opportunities, achieving goals, creating teams, gathering and organizing the necessary resources to get the job done right and on time. Leadership is about communicating your vision, the opportunity or goal you want to achieve so that you can secure the agreement of others who will help you achieve the goal.

Leadership can involve confrontation, but more often it involves resolving conflicts before they eat up too many resources or pit people against each other in a manner that keeps them from working together on the next challenge. Leadership is about having people, including students, work in concern or in unison, and teachers are brilliant at doing this day in and day out. Leadership is about searching for solutions to early stage problems to help solve them before they become big problems.

Leadership is about being efficient by delegating a job to a person who can do it in one hour rather than taking ten hours yourself to attempt to do it. Leadership is sometimes messy and inefficient as stakeholder after stakeholder is included and consulted about key aspects and methods of setting and achieving goals. But, failures of leadership are always messier and even more inefficient.

Recently a school district broke grounds after two years of planning for the building of a school for students who had been expelled from other schools. One of the authors visited the current school where these students were learning and found the students were hard working, the teachers dedicated, and the school building run down and a new school was surely needed. Unfortunately, the school district had never informed the neighbors of their intention to build the school in their neighborhood, and when the construction began on the school, the neighbors were so up in arms, the building of the school was cancelled due to the failure of leadership to enroll the neighbors in the project.

This failure of leadership cost the school district a lot of money, created, unnecessarily, a substantial number of enemies in the neighborhood, and failed to help meet the needs of the students for a more adequate school. Leadership is about getting things done and getting them done in a manner that does not burn out people, does not alienate people, and most importantly, creates goodwill among the stakeholders thus promoting them working together again in the future when the next opportunity or challenge is identified.

Leaders often have to work on many challenges at a time, form many different sets of teams, gather resources from many different sources, stay in communication with many different groups, and maintain a balance in their lives of work, home, physical and emotional well being, and life satisfaction. Knowing the ten simple theories of leadership and ten principles of leadership gives teachers a clearer understanding of leadership.

Since motivation is a key aspect of leadership, we include a brief list of actions leaders undertake to motivate themselves and others around them. This checklist is a small subset of successful leadership approaches. Every leader must learn what work for themselves, and what works for every person or group they lead. Leadership is a dynamic process, and what worked yesterday, may not work tomorrow. However, there are many tried and true activities that are consistently useful as part of the leader's tools and approaches.

LEADERSHIP BEHAVIORS AND MOTIVATION

In order for a teacher to be a better leader, it is useful for the teacher to become familiar with examples of leadership behaviors that have proven successful over time. Within each category and specific behavioral item listed in this chapter, there is great room for individual variations and creativity. However, each of these items listed is relevant for teachers, just as they are relevant for other leaders. There are approximately sixty behaviors that researchers believe constitute good leadership practices.

Checklist 1: People Management

A successful leader is one who:

- Clearly communicates expectations
- Recognizes, acknowledges, and rewards achievement
- Inspires others and serves as a catalyst for others to perform in ways they would not undertake without the leader's support and direction
- Puts the right people in the right positions at the right time with the right resources and right job descriptions
- Secures alignment on what is the right direction for the organization
- Persuades and encourages people in the organization to achieve the desired results for the organization

- Makes sure not to burn out people in the organization, looking out for their well-being as well as the well-being of the organization
- Identifies weak signals that suggest impending conflict within the organization and attacks the sources of conflict effectively
- Holds people accountable
- Encourages the human capital development of every person in the organization through training, mentoring, and education, and allocates sufficient resources to this endeavor
- Correctly evaluates the actual performance and the potential of each person in the organization
- Encourages people in the organization to stand up for and express their beliefs
- Creates a non–fear-based environment in which all persons in the organization can speak the truth as they see it without concern for retaliation
- Is able to empathize with those he or she leads

Checklist 2: Strategic Management

A successful leader is one who:

- Is flexible when necessary to adapt to changing circumstances
- Sets, with input from others including all stakeholders, the long-term direction for the organization
- Understands the organization's competitive environment, social trends, competitors, customers, and all stakeholders
- Correctly analyzes the potential risks of all decisions
- Correctly analyzes the potential returns of all decisions
- Has the ability to focus on specific problems without losing his or her ability to see at the outer edges, gathering worthwhile information that others miss or fail to see as significant or relevant
- Understands the strengths and weaknesses of the organization and how to exploit the strengths and address the weaknesses successfully
- Develops and implements strategies to improve the strengths and to combat the weaknesses of the organization
- Identifies appropriate partners, strategic alliances, and outside resources to tap in order to help further the organization's goals
- Articulates the values of the organization and develops strategies consistent with these core values
- Demonstrates a strong commitment to diversity and positive change
- Demonstrates a strong commitment to creating and sustaining a learning organization (learning is the foundation for all sustainable change)

Checklist 3: Personal Characteristics

A successful leader is one who:

- Lives with honesty and integrity
- Selects people for his or her team who are honest and have high integrity
- Is confident without being arrogant
- Has the will, passion, and desire to succeed
- Possesses a willingness to shoulder the responsibility for success (without being a "thunder taker") and failure (without casting blame)
- Is innovative and open to new ideas
- Is not willing to accept the ways things are because they can always be improved; is never satisfied completely with the status quo
- Is smart, intelligent, emotionally strong
- Is an able negotiator
- Is willing to be patient
- Is decisive when necessary
- Is able to think analytically
- Learns quickly
- Is respectful to all
- Is perceptive and sensitive to the needs of others
- Demonstrates diligence, discipline, and strong perseverance capabilities
- Is comfortable with ambiguity
- Is willing to be original
- Takes informed and intelligent risks

Checklist 4: Process Management

A successful leader is one who:

- Manages change
- Promotes innovation
- Secures resources
- Allocates resources wisely
- Solves problems well
- Anticipates crises
- Handle crises well when they explode
- Creates and manages budgets well
- Creates and manages timelines and work plans
- Possesses and manifests great project management skills
- Translates long-term visions into step-by-step plans
- Measures results and reports them accurately

- Recognizes quickly when a process or activity is not working
- Redesigns processes as often as necessary to be successful

MOTIVATION EXPLAINED AND DEMONSTRATED

Literature from as far back as 1974 provides some useful guidance on motivating oneself and others. House and Mitchell in their article "***Path-Goal Theory of Leadership***" state that leadership generates motivation when the leaders show that he or she has the power and influence to improve situations and undertakes the following behaviors:

1. Is willing and able to increase the kinds of payoffs that subordinates want
2. Shows willingness to create rapport with subordinates
3. Works to make the subordinates' jobs easier and more likely to be successful
4. Makes sacrifices on behalf of subordinates
5. Gives acknowledgement appropriately
6. Creates goals and objectives that are intrinsically appealing to subordinates

Twenty-two factors below help in creating an environmental where leaders can be effective in motivating those they lead.

1. Subordinates understand the goals of the group and its leaders.
2. Subordinates know what is expected of them.
3. Leaders maintain a friendly yet disciplined relationship with subordinates.
4. Leaders consult with subordinates.
5. Leaders coach and mentor subordinates.
6. Leaders listen actively to subordinates.
7. Lead ers keep subordinates accurately informed.
8. Leaders exhibit the same ethics they demand of subordinates and are trusted by subordinates.
9. Leaders endeavor to understand the situation the subordinates face.
10. Leaders set realistic individual and collective goals for subordinates and challenge subordinates in a way that engenders strong, positive responses.
11. Leaders take into account the feelings and emotions of subordinates and try to accommodate their personal needs.
12. Leaders give encouragement to subordinates.
13. Leaders help subordinates become better problem solvers.

14. Leaders tell the truth to subordinates and demand the same from them.
15. Leaders deliver punishment effectively when warranted.
16. Leaders are perceived by subordinates as being fair.
17. Leaders create a vision for subordinates and peers that is realistic, comprehensible, and challenges their imagination.
18. Leaders use humor appropriately.
19. Leaders express appropriate confidence in subordinates.
20. Leaders know the capabilities of their subordinates, demand that they perform at their highest levels, and let subordinates know that the leader is monitoring their activities against that standard.
21. Leaders undertake substantial effort to help subordinates grow into leaders.
22. Leaders resign when they fail or when their subordinates are not motivated to success by the leader's actions, thus allowing another leader to take the reins.

Certainly, being able to motivate oneself and others requires additional important attributes, including the following:

1. Recognizing and avoiding burnout in oneself and others
2. Improving the ability of participants to delegate and achieve results through the work and cooperation of others
3. Articulating and understanding group dynamics, followership, and factors in communications styles, strategies, and content that affect the response of others
4. Recognizing the power of building long-lasting professional relationships
5. Implementing strategies to create and elicit rapport
6. Appreciating the value of one's reputation and its relationship to motivation
7. Calling forth the leadership potential in others and in oneself
8. Knowing the role of fair and equitable treatment of others in achieving and maintaining high motivation

CONCLUSION

Leadership theory and motivation are critical components of leadership. Teachers are called upon every day to motivate students, assistants, school administrators, and most importantly, themselves. Burnout is a function of a decrease of motivation, more than it is a function of being worn out due to excessive work. Avoiding burnout is essential for teachers and this chapter has included information and theories that are designed to guide teachers for the long run who want to be better leaders.

No one who wants to be a better leader need memorize all ten theories and all ten principles of leadership. No one has to begin to undertake all of the activities that support motivation right away. These checklists are good guideposts for leadership development. As teachers become better leaders, these types of activities will become more and more natural and will yield significant results.

Chapter 6

The Potential for Improved Leadership by Teachers to Achieve Systemic Change in PreK–12 Education

THE HISTORICAL CONTEXT FOR LEADERSHIP FOR TEACHERS

It is important to acknowledge that although few teachers receive leadership development training, there have been many who have advocated this before. There have been books, articles, conferences, and working papers on school reform, especially from the 1990s, and the role that improving the leadership identity, skills, and activities of teachers could contribute to this reform.

The work of Joseph Murphy has documented this work brilliantly and has furthered it considerably. Work by ETS today is seeking to define teacher leadership in a new manner. Work by the Educational Commission for the States is also delving into how improving the ability of teachers will improve schools and create systemic change in PreK–12 education.

Teachers as leaders, as described in this book, is somewhat different from some of the earlier literature on this topic, but builds on this body of work. Schools have made great strides in instructional leadership, while our teachers have made fewer strides developing their own leadership abilities. We have outlined a new and expanded role for students and teachers in schools throughout this book. Improved leadership skills of teachers will yield a new domain in schools that cannot yet be defined.

SYSTEMIC CHANGE IN SCHOOLS

Leadership creates followers. Therefore, it is likely that as teachers become better leaders, they will gain even more followers in the community than they now have. It is also likely that as teachers become better leaders, they will have even greater student appreciation, and parent appreciation, than they have today. Since we have called for teachers, acting as leaders, to do more in the way of peer mentoring and counseling, as teachers become better leaders, we expect they will have even more appreciation from their peers than they have today.

Further, as teachers become better leaders, we expect over time that teachers and administrators will view each other more and more as partners, and less and less as people who operate on different levels in the school system. Teachers, as they become better leaders, may be more willing to go out into the community and speak on behalf of the school to the Rotary Clubs and other service clubs.

Leaders are those who investigate and learn new technologies to the best of their abilities. We can see how improved leadership skills for teachers will translate into a greater willingness and ability to embrace and learn new technologies that may be both time saving to teachers, and enhance the student learning experience. There is much in new information technology that can aid schools and teachers need to be trained in this new technology.

HELPING TEACHERS FIND THEIR VOICE IN SCHOOL IMPROVEMENT EFFORTS

This book is about voice. As better leaders, teachers will become even more vocal in demanding the type of training that they believe will help improve student outcomes and help improve their lives as teachers. We see teachers, as they become better leaders, also becoming more innovative with technology in the school and having the leadership skill attempt to learn new technologies that seem today to be out of their reach. We see teachers, as they become better leaders, using their voice to help bring about changes in schools that they believe will improve their schools.

That is the sign of leadership. Leaders define and shape their roles and they select the tools they believe will best serve them. Leaders decide what tools and technologies they use.

It is the job of a leader to do the hard stuff. Principals and school board members have not been as successful as they would like in getting higher and higher percentages of students to graduate or getting more parents on board with helping in the education of their children.

Teachers, acting as leaders, can come up with more ideas, spoken with a stronger voice, on how to improve the percentage of students graduating from high school, and they can be even more effective in enrolling parents as partners in the educational process. Teachers, with enhanced leadership skills, can help enroll volunteers from the community to participate effectively in our schools. Certainly there are issues with having more volunteers from the community help out in our PreK–12 schools, but these issues can be resolved.

IMPROVING LEADERSHIP CAPABILITIES OF TEACHERS IMPACTS THE COMMUNITY

Teachers, with better leadership skills, can help resolve these issues, put out a call to the community for volunteers, and can help recruit and lead these volunteers to becoming an effective part of the school experience. One of the authors of this book contacted a school board chairman of a Colorado school district and volunteered to help recruit volunteers for schools from the community. He was not called back by the school board chairman who was focusing her time, and possibly rightly so, on budget cuts.

When the school board does not lead, and when administrators do not lead on such issues as increasing resources, including volunteers from the community, to help PreK–12 schools, then teachers, with enhanced leadership skills, must step forward to lead. Systematic change often does not start at the top. It starts with people with a clear vision for the future. This is why it is so important for teachers to begin to create a "vision" with other teachers about how to change their schools.

RESET—THE NEW ADVANCED FORM OF CHANGE

In fact, the key word today is not "change" at all. It is "reset." School reform movements have contributed to significant improvement in schools. School reform movements seek to make changes in schools. Today, some things, including some schools, need more than mere change.

They need to be reset and it is our view that when "resets" become a function of teachers acting as level four leaders, that schools will be much more able to reach their potential and assist their students in reaching their potential. Teachers can play a significant role in this "resetting" process. A reset is a much more profound "change" than what we normally call "change." It is a significant departure, taken in one step, or one leap, to move a school or other institution, closer to its vision and its goals.

This book has made the argument that we need to establish leadership at levels one, two, three, and four, as a key competency for teachers. Librarians in 1998 and their associations reset the standards for the profession of library science to embrace leadership. It is now time for teachers and all of their associations, journals, unions, and organized groups to reset the competencies for teachers to include and embrace leadership.

Since this book is about teachers, we know that as teachers begin to act individually and in concert with each other, they can change (and even help "reset") schools more than they are currently changing our schools. They can help transform our schools more effectively than they are able to do so today. They can embrace technology more effectively than they do today, so that even though many of our schools were built in the last century, the students can benefit from this century's latest information technology available on the market.

LEADERSHIP DEVELOPMENT REQUIRES PATIENCE AND PERSERVERENCE

We know that teachers cannot change everything overnight. But we also know that today more teachers, if properly trained in leadership development, can act as level four leaders, can create a plan to change schools significantly, and can help make their plan, their vision, a reality. This book starts with the teacher just becoming a better leader of themselves (level one), then a better leader in their classrooms, then a better leader in dealing with other teachers and administrators, then parents, and then a better leader dealing with the schools as an organization and the outside community. As teachers help other teachers become better leaders, they will become more effective as a group in helping produce better student outcomes and improving our schools.

There is no simple formula for how to get this done, although this book includes exercises and ideas that can be put in place by teachers to move along this dimension and leadership improvement track quite quickly. The starting point is commitment to success in the endeavor. Teachers work hard. Leadership helps people accomplish more, often without more effort.

IMPROVING TEACHERS' LEADERSHIP ABILITIES WILL RESULT IN MORE SUPPORT

We are not asking teachers for more effort. We are asking teachers to lead more and, when they do, their influence on schools, students, the community, the resources made available to education in the United States, and the public support for education in the United States will increase substantially. This is our prediction.

The results will depend on the quality of leadership that individual teachers and groups of teachers can attain. We have confidence that the 3,663,000 PreK–12 teachers in the United States can all become more effective leaders in their schools.

THE ESSENTIAL ROLE OF SHARING YOUR LEADERSHIP DEVELOPMENT WORK

We also encourage teachers to share with other teachers and school personnel why and how improving the leadership qualities of teachers is an important way to improve schools. Undertaking these activities need not be done alone. There are many people out there to support teachers as seek to become better leaders as long as teachers let them know of their commitment to become better leaders. That is why undertaking all of these exercises and not letting other teachers, parents, school personnel, and the community know of this new leadership development movement among teachers is a surefire way to limit the effectiveness of these exercises and to limit the effectiveness of teachers, as a whole, as leaders.

CONCLUSION

Our next and final chapter includes leadership development activities that teachers can work with and work on every day. There are hundreds of potential exercises and activities that our teachers could begin to undertake to strengthen their leadership muscles. Many teachers may have already thought of and begun practicing many of them. We urge teachers to use the activities that are most relevant to each individual teacher and each school setting.

The leadership development activities in Chapter Seven are followed by a series of leadership development exercises in Appendix B that give teachers many avenues to become a better leader. Teachers should on a regular basis select a few leadership development exercises and set aside time to invest in becoming a better leader. The rewards of being a better leader will bring new opportunities to teachers, new improvements to your school, and contribute to students, their parents, and the overall community.

Leadership development for teachers can plan a key role in systemic change and improvements for schools. It is now time for teachers to expand their leadership capabilities. The work and exercises in the next chapter will guide teachers along this path and can play a key role in changing our schools for the better.

Chapter 7

Ten Steps Teachers can Take to Improve their Leadership Capacity and their Schools

GOALS OF THE BOOK

This book has two related goals. First is for each and every PreK–12 teacher to recognize that every teacher is a leader. Second, it is the goal of this book to assist all teachers to improve your leadership skills. The payoffs may not be obvious at first, but a list of payoffs that you can reasonably expect from improving your leadership skills include:

- improving your ability to manage and plan your time
- improve your ability to obtain the resources you need to perform your job in an excellent manner
- have greater satisfaction in your teaching career and in your life
- obtaining better respect and discipline from your students
- improving your ability to help students achieve better educational outcomes
- improved relations with parents, peers, administrators, support staff, librarians, and coaches
- increasing your confidence
- a better ability to define your role and activities in life, rather than have the circumstances and people around you define, confine and control your roles and activities in life

These are some of the benefits of improving your leadership skills. In school settings or in any organizational setting, leadership is rarely, if ever, done best if it is a solo act. Leadership is best performed when it is a standard operating premise of many people in an organization. When one teacher acts as a leader, it sends a signal to other teachers that leadership is not only an option for teachers it is also the best approach to your job. Leadership requires training and practice. In this book we have provided teachers, in a concise and easily accessible format, a solid foundation in leadership theory, leadership best practices, and shown over and over how teachers are leaders.

Some have come before us with this message, teachers are leaders. But, overall, in the teaching profession, this message does not come through to teachers. In fact, the opposite message comes through much more strongly. Teachers day in and day out are told what to teach on what day and what test for which to prepare their students. This book flies in the face of the harsh reality that our school systems have often not viewed teachers as leaders and have worked hard to prevent teachers from learning leadership development or exercising their true skills as leaders.

This book is about getting the message directly to teachers throughout our nation: Teachers are leaders. Become better leaders and teaching, career satisfaction, effectiveness, and schools will improve significantly.

From the first quote by President Obama in this book, "The time to expand the promise of education is now," to this concluding chapter, our message has been consistent. We are not asking teachers to remake themselves in some completely new way to become leaders. Teachers are already leaders, and deep down, as students look to teachers day in and day out to be their leader, teachers know teachers are leaders.

We are not asking teachers to devote hours to yet another unpaid set of tasks that will lead to nowhere. Reading this book and starting to perform the exercises in this book, can all begin in one week. The most important word in President Obama's statement at the beginning of this book about the realizing the potential of education is his use of the word "now."

Now is the time to accept the mantle of leader and act consistent with its ideals and the opportunities it presents. Leadership starts with each teacher, not a principal even where they exist who want teachers to become better leaders. As teachers become more aware that teachers are leaders, and as teachers undertake exercises and training in leadership (as librarians have done since 1998 on a regular basis), teachers will inevitably have an impact on other teachers who want to become better leaders.

Teachers will increase what we have referred to as "leadership density" in schools and in the other organizations where teachers participate in the community. Leadership density sits at the core of organizational effectiveness and school reform. Principals, educational consultants, authors, and trainers can help teachers with instructional strategies, curriculum alignment, classroom management, lesson planning, and numerous other aspects of teaching.

If, however, teachers in concert with all other key actors in schools fail to help develop leadership abilities among teachers and the staff, educational initiatives to improve schools and student outcomes will have a poor chance of being implemented effectively or will not be sustained. Michael Fullan goes further. He states:

> There is no chance that large-scale reform will happen, let alone stick, unless capacity building is a central component of the strategy for improvement. (*Leadership and Sustainability*, 2005)

Every teacher is a leader and has the potential to become a better leader. The most effective principals and superintendents will work hard to encourage leadership among teachers and establish the conditions for teachers' true leadership potential to be exercised each and every day in numerous ways in the educational setting. At the same time, teachers must know that this book is a call to action on their part, because the development of anyone's leadership abilities cannot rely on the will of education's "titled" leaders.

Leadership development starts with the individual's will to be a leader and to identify him or herself as a leader, a worthy leader. Leadership ability is generated and revealed through action and therefore must be practiced. While this book and other manuals for leadership can help guide the teacher intent on growing his or her capacity, a teacher can only grow leadership competency by acting as a leader.

Not every leadership activity will succeed. Some leadership activities will be strongly opposed by those who believe their own leadership turf is being threatened. So be it. Over time, true leaders learn to work well, even brilliantly, with other leaders. Insecure leaders, fight tooth and nail to preserve their leadership turf, but eventually, lose the fight because of the huge amount of energy it takes to fight off other leaders who outnumber them sometimes 10 or 100 to 1.

So, the path to success is never guaranteed for anyone embarking on leadership, but the path itself is so much more rewarding for those who pave it with leadership, that the journey is always worth more than the effort. In this book we have also tried to demystify leadership. Leadership is about first being a leader in all things where you can guide your life to be more effective and more efficient, more resourceful, and more successful.

In every teacher's life, there are many areas improving leadership skills will lead directly to an increase in effectiveness in solving problems, addressing challenges, avoiding burnout, and maintaining optimism and enthusiasm. Leadership involves taking effective action and making or helping to make more effective decisions. Leadership is not only about making major decisions it is also about the small, purposeful acts that improve performance in the classroom, and in life in general. Leadership is about assisting others in performing better at your school. Leadership is about the small, purposeful acts that improve how each organization in which teachers participate, including schools, school districts, extracurricular activities, and community organizations. Leadership is about becoming more aware of one's strengths and weaknesses (level one), about understanding the perspective of others and helping others make sense of new information (level two), about inspiring others and helping others grow (level three), and about participating in a common, organization wide cause, and acting with integrity (level four).

We started the book with three words—teachers are leaders. Our job is to ask teachers throughout this nation to accept that mantle. Where teachers have already accepted this mantle before ever reading this book, we request that those teachers who are already leaders work every day to become an even better leader.

Indeed, the most effective organizations are the ones in which the majority of those not in the highest rungs of the pecking order carry out small, but significant and purposeful acts of leadership every day. Every teacher can take immediate steps to improve their leadership capacity, to practice the art of leadership.

In this concluding chapter, we share our ten best recommendations for assisting you to improve as a leader. These actions do require some time to undertake. Yet, they are designed to promote teachers working together in a way that does not leave teachers vulnerable in any way. These activities and the ones that follow in the Appendices are designed to give teachers energy rather than take energy. They are designed help teachers become more effective and efficient.

Hopefully, success in performing these activities will actually give teachers more time due to their becoming more efficient and better at delegating and enrolling others to provide needed assistance. We know that teachers' days, evenings, and weekends are filled with school-related work, and time is something which teachers do not have much to give. Most importantly, we have designed these activities in a manner that every teacher is fully capable of undertaking. We admit, these ten steps require initiative, and they require teachers to begin to identify and act as leaders, but they are doable for every teacher in America.

TEN STEPS TOWARD BECOMING A
BETTER LEADER IN SCHOOLS

1) Seek Feedback From Peers and Others

One of the ways to do this is to create a buddy group or circle of friends who are teachers. Ask two or three other teachers to commit to observing each other teach, work with students, meet with parents, speak in public or participate in meetings, get organized for a class, and other key activities that teachers perform on a regular basis.

The group should have members observe one another ideally several times, and at least once a month. Then the member observing the other member, in private, should give feedback to the teacher who was observed. Then the group should hold a monthly meeting to discuss what each learned from observing and from the feedback. This way, when one person in the group learns something, it is likely that every person in the group will learn something.

This constructive feedback must be honest and always given with the intention of assisting the other person and all persons in the group, become better leaders. No teacher will always agree with all of the feedback, but almost all of it will prove to be useful in some way. Use a rubric or template to help keep the feedback focused on those things that will help all teachers improve their leadership skills.

This activity will help teachers assess their strengths and areas for growth in an informal setting. It will help develop self-awareness, which is a key aspect of level one leadership. This activity will naturally spread to asking other teachers, parents and students, staff, principals, family members, and friends for feedback on a more regular basis.

2) Assess Your Current Leadership Capacity and Establish a Leadership Growth Goal

Use the leadership rubric provided in Chapter Two of this book to conduct a self-assessment. Be as honest and assess yourself as accurately as possible. Once you have conducted the self-assessment, create a specific goal to improve in at least one area of the rubric. This act of self-assessment and goal setting also helps one develop level one leadership.

This exercise which should take no more than one hour, should be repeated several times during the year to chart your progress. You can even ask others to give you their viewpoints on this assessment. When done systematically in organizations where superiors and subordinates do this assessment of others, it is called 360 feedback and has proven to be very useful to help people understand how others view them.

3) Practice Gaining Perspective or Demonstrating a Sense of Perspective at a Staff Meeting

At the next staff meeting, make a comment or ask a question using the words "point of view" or "perspective" in your remarks. Consider using any of the following examples:

"I agree with your *perspective* on the need for _____, and I would add . . ."

"The notion that _____ is an understandable *point of view.* I wonder . . ."

"You provide an important *perspective.* Perhaps we should also consider . . ."

If you are not used to speaking up in meetings, this leadership act may seem somewhat contrived at first. Still, conducting this leadership action will not only force you to listen for the perspective of others it will also demonstrate to others that you are actively listening and trying to gain understanding.

4) Job Shadow an Administrator

Usually teachers shadow an administrator only if they plan to be in administration. Level two leadership, however, requires everyone to understand the goals and priorities of the organization and the decision-making structure. In other words, you will be a better teacher and a stronger teacher leader if you understand the larger picture of the organization.

Find an assistant principal, principal, or central office administrator who would be willing to let you shadow them for a day or even one-half of a day. Job shadow the administrator, taking note of decisions made, major areas of focus, and topics of conversations with other people. At the end of the day, debrief with the administrator to gain greater understanding of the decisions made and the type of activities in which the administrator engaged.

Afterwards, and on your own, reflect on these three questions:

- Which leadership skills and actions (from the leadership framework) were exhibited by the administrator?
- Which leadership skills and actions were demonstrated by the staff members during the day?
- What decisions would you have made differently and why?

5) Teach Your Colleagues

Leaders continue to learn and also contribute to the knowledge of others. Find a current area of interest that also impacts a reform initiative or an improvement area for your school or district. This area might even include improving leadership skills of teachers. Then work with your organization's "titled leaders" to organize and implement an opportunity to teach a handful of other teachers and/or staff members, or even a larger number to teach this new skill or facilitate a discussion on this topic.

As a leader, you can even organize a structure where these types of teaching sessions happen on a regular basis, weekly or monthly, at a scheduled time, and you can work with others to help set the agendas, ideas or topics that will be discussed and planned over time. If you are not used to presenting to or teaching peers, you might start off this aspect of leadership by co-teaching or co-presenting.

The important point to remember is that once you get beyond level one leadership, leadership behavior begins to shift from a focus on one's own ability to that of the larger group.

6) Make a Habit of Complimenting Others on a Valued Behavior

Leaders motivate. One does not have to be a motivational speaker in order to inspire. More often than not, it is the small, but sincere compliment or pat on the back that inspires people to do their best work. Make a habit of extending a compliment to a colleague, subordinate, or supervisor regarding a positive behavior that you observed.

The behaviors you want to compliment as a leader are the ones valued by the organization to meet the goals or objectives of the organization. Teachers are brilliant at this practice when it comes to their students. They regularly compliment students on valued behavior. Seek ways to compliment students that you have not regularly complimented in the past.

The valued behavior could be a small thing, like one student picking up a pen or pencil for another student. It does not need to be making a 100 on the hardest test of the month. The next step would be to expand this habit of acknowledgement to everyone, not just students and other teachers.

Complimenting others has four distinct leadership developmental benefits for teachers. First, it shows others that you have noticed them doing something right and they appreciate being noticed for doing something right. When others increase their appreciation of you, they look to you more favorably as someone who is capable of leading them. Second, it trains leaders to look hard and broadly for signs that people are doing valued things. Searching broadly actually expands our "peripheral" vision and allows us to include more people in what we see in life.

Leaders have a great ability to have a broad spectrum of vision that includes many people and many activities simultaneously. Third, it gives people energy when you notice them doing things right and increases their appreciation of life. Leaders need a lot of energy and leaders know they have to create the energy within themselves and others, and this is a great way to add to your energy and the energy of people around you.

Fourth, complimenting others for valued behavior shows them that you have high standards and appreciate when they are met. Leaders have high standards, high expectations of themselves, and of others. When you compliment others, they understand that you are sharing your standards with them and that they meet your standards. There can be no more direct way to show approval and at the same time establish yourself as a leader who cares about the people you lead.

7) Help Someone Make Sense of a Policy or Practice

Leaders not only communicate but they also help make sense of new information or a new policy. We grant you that not all of the policies that teachers have to follow these days make sense. However, before one criticizes out of hand any policy it is very important to search for the reasons behind the policy and see if it makes sense. Often, you will discover two important leadership development ideas out of this practice.

First, leaders always seek to understand before they criticize. Second, there is usually some rational basis for the policy, even if it is not the best policy. Once you understand the basis for a policy, two great opportunities emerge. First, you can share that understanding with others and encourage them to look more deeply into why the policy was generated in the first place.

Second, once you and your colleague understand why the policy or practice was generated, you may have some insights into how a better policy or practice can fix the situation and will be well-equipped to help initiate or participate in future discussions on improving the policy or practice. This is what leaders do. They see a situation, seek to understand its origins, seek to understand how others have responded to it, and often offer and advocate for a different response that will better resolve or address the situation.

This approach should become a habit to be evoked whenever there is a new policy or practice, school reform, change or new information that goes through your school. Understand the basis. Seek out opportunities to do sense-making. When such an opportunity arises, practice asking yourself and processing with others the following:

- Are you getting accurate information or only part of the picture?
- Do you understand the information? What is the context?
- What clarification or additional information do you still need to make an informed judgment?
- Whose perspective and what interests should you consider while formulating your own reaction and before relaying the information as presented?
- In what ways can you explain the rationale for the change, action, requirement, etc.?
- How might you build perspective—an appreciation for the bigger picture or the interests of other individuals, groups, or organizations?

- Do you have ideas on how to improve the situation that are better than the currently proposed or implemented solution?
- Is there a way to communicate your ideas that will actually help improve the policy or practice, or the information you are receiving?
- Can you encourage others who agree with you to assist you in communicating this new, better approach?

Making sense of information does not mean that you have to agree with the plan, policy, requirement, or decision. It is incumbent upon every leader at every level to seek understanding and to appreciate various perspectives before making a judgment. Being purposeful about sense-making will help expand your level three leadership and give you the firm basis upon which to think about how to help improve the situation, the essential goal of every leader.

8) Mentor an Inexperienced or Struggling Teacher

Volunteer to help a new teacher or even an experienced colleague who wants to grow in the profession. This mentoring can be done formally or informally. Many schools have an official mentoring program for new teachers or teachers on improvement plans. Find out about becoming a mentor.

Once you make a decision to do this, your ability to see that other teachers are struggling will grow. In fact, once you gain a reputation as a teacher who assists other teachers in a very effective manner, other teachers who are struggling will seek you out. If done right, they will not be a drain on you. You, as a leader and mentor, will begin to see patterns of challenges first, and patterns of solutions to those challenges.

You will be able to more and more quickly diagnose challenges and more and more quickly dispense ideas, solutions or help those who ask you for mentoring and coaching, to discover the solutions that are right for them. The more you mentor and observe these evolving patterns of challenges and solutions (often called "best practices") the more quality leadership information you will gain, and the more your ability to gain perspective will grow.

While this mentoring is designed to contribute in a meaningful way to others, it will contribute to your leadership abilities in a significant way. As a leader you will learn that some whom you mentor will not follow your advice and some will. As a leader you will find and develop communication strategies that are more and more effective in getting those to whom you give advice to at least try it and give you feedback as to whether the advice worked or not.

Sometimes, those you mentor will share with you an approach they discovered and you as a leader will learn something important about an approach about which you had not been aware. Regardless of the availability of official mentoring positions, one can always offer support to another colleague. Providing support to a colleague can be done in a number of innocuous ways. Consider the following examples:

- Designing and sharing a lesson plan
- Modeling a lesson or instructional strategy
- Asking a teacher to join you in a book study
- Recommending a particularly useful resource
- Sharing classroom management procedures
- Offering to co-teach a lesson with another teacher
- Designing a scoring rubric with others

Mentoring or providing support for others is part of level three leadership. This leadership activity helps develop your coaching abilities. One has to practice being a coach to become an even stronger leader.

9) Offer a Solution to a Significant Problem or Challenge or Help Create a Goal or Vision.

Take an issue that is affecting more than one person and study it and begin to craft what you believe would be a useful solution to the problem. This problem or challenge could be a school-wide issue or concern, it could be an issue that students have raised, or parents have raised, or could be an issue that has been in the press regarding your school or school district. The issue can be relatively big or small. It actually does not matter.

Teachers are leaders who with sufficient study and investigation can tackle big issues and well as moderate size issues. You do not have to start with a small issue for practice. Rather, start out with an issue that interests you and energizes you and, if solved properly, will likely produce a strong benefit or positive result. When you develop your understanding of the issue and begin to develop a solution, begin to check with those you trust and discuss the issue and your suggested approach.

Others often can build on your ideas quickly and make excellent suggestions for improving your good solution and then you will have an even better solution than if you had gone forward to present your solution without first discussing it with trusted colleagues. When you present a solution where others have helped you form that solution, they will be your strongest supporters and you will be in the position of "leader" of them on that issue.

This action to be successful will require you to research the issue effectively, gaining accurate information about the issue and the people who are either currently creating the problem or trying to solve it. Behind every issue or problem there are people, and knowing where the people stand on the issue, and how these people are trying to be influential on this issue is essential for a person to know how to begin to understand the situation and to fashion a solution that will work. Also, it is important to get information directly from the people involved in the situation and investigate their various perspectives, and consider their different interests.

Then, as you begin to frame your "solution," begin to assess the benefits and costs of your own solution compared to the current "solution." Using this problem-solving approach, combined with gathering input and support from others, are all good practices for a leader. The level three leader uses a problem-solving approach when faced with a challenge.

One of the organizational challenges schools and departments face is the self-imposed limits to problem solving that many teachers set. Teachers sometimes sit back and watch the titled leaders come up with the answers, allowing themselves to be led instead of exercising leadership themselves. While some supervisors may feel that even the proffering of a suggestion by a teacher is somehow overstepping bounds, most are more receptive to solutions presented in a professional way.

In any case, it is the responsibility of the teacher who wants to be a better leader to provide input and become part of solving the key concerns of the school or organization. It is important to know what the real institutional constraints are in injecting yourself into either the "input" (fact finding) or the "decision making" process. There are real constraints and carved out areas where a teacher cannot go. This is understood. However, there are also "perceived" constraints that are often manifested in such statements by others or even yourself as, "You better not do that," "So and so won't like it if you do that," "If you do that, it will cost you," and so on.

Sometimes these statements turn out to be true, but often they are false. Leaders push the edge to see how far they can get into the "input" process or in the "decision" making process. Leaders always pursue the investigative or fact searching process and leaders are often amazed about how successful they are at "getting to the bottom" of the situation after a careful investigation. Once a person really gets to the bottom of a situation and knows what has happened and why it has happened, it is usually the case that this person is allowed input into future decisions that will be made on the subject.

The person probably may not become the decision maker, but having input into the process is the most surefire way to having "influence" on the decision. Leaders should not back down from false walls, false constraints, false threats, false definitions or roles by others to keep teachers down or from participating as leaders. Leaders always challenge the boundaries and try to form "teams" so they can participate at the "team" level.

The entire PreK–12 teaching profession is uniquely suited to helping each other in the teaching profession become a better leader. This book is designed to be a catalyst that speeds up this process of teachers becoming better leaders. This activity, offering a solution to a challenge, after careful investigation, works at:

- the individual level
- the small group level
- the school level
- the school district level
- the state level
- the education profession level
- the national level
- at the world level

This activity of offering a solution to a problem should not be viewed as either successful or a failure depending on whether your exact solution is implemented. Pursuing the process of deciding to offer a solution, doing the investigation, giving input, seeking to influence the decision, all build leadership muscles, skills and aptitude. Simply pursuing this activity will make you a better leader.

One goal of this activity is that as a teacher and as a leader you will train yourself to look for solutions, while others merely see problems. You will naturally begin to try and figure out a solution that will not only resolve this challenge but also prevent this or a similar type of problem from happening again. Teachers do this every minute in the classroom. Teachers are amazing problem solvers.

Having 20 to 30 PreK–12 students all in a classroom setting at one time trying to learn something is an open invitation to many interactions in a given minute and problems arise every day, every hour in the classroom and educational setting. We know that teachers are great problem solvers. They do it every day and use many approaches to solving problems. We urge teachers to use their excellent problem solving skills to tackle challenges that they see where they see that others are not stepping up to provide a good solution.

It is the leadership viewpoint that "I am a leader" that will more strongly than any other viewpoint lead teachers to become better and better problem solvers and be willing to help address tougher and tougher problems and challenges.

10) Help Develop a Picture of What Success Looks Like

Leaders develop and refine their idea of what success looks like. When one goal is reached, another one is put in place to guide activity. Goals become milestones, not destinations. Success becomes the minimal acceptable result and not the achievement that lets people believe they deserve a crown and the right to just sit on the throne.

Goals, objectives, and success metrics (identifiable, documentable, provable measures of success) are often described as "key performance indicators" by leaders of organizations. Key performance indicators are the descriptions of the behaviors that leaders believe will help them and those around them achieve their goals in a timely and efficient manner. The purpose of having goals, at the individual and at the organizational level, is to help create a "vision" of what true success will look like. Leaders are always refining their visions for themselves and at the organizational level, always assisting others in organizations move toward a shared vision.

Again, one doesn't have to be the principal or district leader in order to develop that shared vision and to help people aspire to it. At a practical level, helping to accomplish a larger vision usually means translating that vision into specific actions that describe what success or excellence looks like. Teachers who want to be better leaders can start in almost any situation by asking the question: "What is our vision of success here?" While that question can stop almost any meeting in its tracks for a moment, it is the place from which leaders begin to shape the future.

One never has to have a "titled leadership position" to ask that question. Leaders consistently improve their skills at taking the opportunity to help others develop a picture of excellence or a picture of what success looks like. This leadership act also can be accomplished in multiple ways right in the school setting by teachers. For example:

- Take one objective or criterion from the teacher evaluation instrument and help design a rubric that describes that objective in specific, observable behaviors.
- Take a teacher skill such as student-teacher engagement and develop a training DVD that shows what great engagement looks like.
- Conduct action research to identify best practices with regard to a school reform initiative.
- Initiate a distinguished teacher certification program in your school or district.
- Organize a leadership academy for teachers to help others learn what leadership looks like at the teacher level.

CONCLUSION

These exercises and activities can be done in any order and at any time. We invite all teachers to create additional exercises and activities and send them to us at www.leadershipforteachers.com. The goal is to pursue improving your leadership abilities each month, each week, and each day. Summer, if you are not teaching, is a great time for a more intensive effort to improve your leadership skills. Ultimately, this book is about making a significant change in the teachers whose hard work has made our school system as good as it is today, and whose newly developed leadership skills can make our schools as good as they can be within the next decade.

Conclusion

Teachers are leaders. Every leader is at times a leader and at times a follower. No one can be a leader at every moment, and when leadership is spread out with people at all "levels" taking leadership initiative, no one person or group should ever try to lead everything all of the time.

This book is designed to assist teachers and our valiant PreK–12 educational system operate at a more effective level in the future. Every sector, every industry, every group, including teachers, must strive for improvement. The number of teachers quitting this most important profession is unacceptable. The number of teachers who do think of themselves as leaders is unacceptable.

The performance of and enthusiasm of our students in our schools is unacceptable. The perception of how our schools are preparing our students for the next generation of jobs and challenges is unacceptable. The level of resources that many of our schools have and many of our teachers get paid is unacceptable. School reform has come and gone and comes again as an overarching approach to improving schools. For most people schools are buildings and buildings are not reformed very easily.

For us, schools are teachers and students. Our view of the world is simple. Teachers lead students. That is why we have devoted this book to you, the teacher. Developing and improving yourself as leader begins with a small step, a few spoken words, that over time become not just what you do, or leadership acts, but who you are—a leader. The few spoken words are, "I am a leader." "I am a teacher because I am a leader." And, "I am a leader, because I am a teacher."

There never should have been any separation between the identity of a teacher and the identity of a leader. Teachers = Leaders. And as our teachers taught us in elementary school math, due the associative principle of mathematics, if Teachers = Leaders, then Leaders = Teachers.

Since Teachers = Leaders, it is time for the educational associations, the school boards, the school district superintendents, the parents, the government leaders in education and the teachers, and every stakeholder to begin to demand that teachers be given leadership training and treated with the dignity that leaders deserve. Whether the education profession chooses to use this book or any book, video, wiki, training course, or other instructional device, that is not what is important.

What is important is that the time is now to expand the promise of education and to do that we must now begin to expand the leadership capabilities and leadership skills and competencies of the most important asset we have in education, our teachers. Starting today, all teachers can become better leaders. Teachers can lead other teachers to become better leaders. Teachers can demand that all schools who certify and train teachers have leadership courses as core courses in that certification process.

Teachers can demand that all teachers receive, as a matter of right, leadership training at no expense to the teachers except the time they will devote to the training. Teachers, since leadership always starts with you and your own group, can demand that every teacher become better trained in leadership, practice leadership more diligently, learn more about leadership, and continuously encourage each other teacher and yourself to act as a leader.

Teachers, starting today, can stand in front of classrooms and your own mirrors and begin to know in a new way that you are a leader. Teachers can give themselves and demand from others the dignity and respect that leaders deserve. Teachers can, starting today, begin working every day in every classroom to help develop the leadership skills of your students, as these leadership skills for them will be vitally important in the twenty-first century, just as the knowledge and technical skills they will receive in PreK–12 classrooms.

Leadership development for students in PreK–12 lets students begin to learn and formulate the knowledge of "what to do" in life, while traditional education and vocational training focuses primarily on letting students know "how to do it." There is much leadership development work day in and day out with students. When one of the authors asked a renowned PreK teacher, Perry Carre, of Stoddert Elementary School in Washington, D.C., whether she thought there was any role for teaching leadership in PreK class to her students, she responded by saying, "That is all I teach in PreK—how to work and learn and play together; how to help others and be willing to be helped by others."

For Perry Carre and for many teachers, coaches, librarians, special educational teachers, and extracurricular activity supervisors, who have devoted their careers to looking not only for that "teachable moment" but also that "leadership development" moment, we applaud you and hope you will share your best strategies for helping students and other teachers become better leaders with your other teachers.

Teachers will be the prime movers of every improvement in our public educational system in the United States. It will not come from one government leader, although government leaders can provide more needed resources to our schools. Americans, once they experience our teachers as the leaders they are and can be, and can see the improvements that teachers can bring to bear on our educational system and the educational outcomes of students, will be more willing to vote for those bond issues they have been turning down recently with great regularity.

In the "nonprofit" world, as all great nonprofit leaders know, "money follows leadership." We predict that better leadership development of teachers will improve student outcomes, teacher satisfaction, reduce teacher turnover, increase the number of people who want to become teachers, and improve parent and community relations with teachers. Students who have been cutting class and performing poorly may start showing up more often for class—not because President Obama says that quitting school is not an option—but because they will know that they have the opportunity to be in the presence of a leader who can make their life better if they just listen to and learn from that leader. That leader is you, the teacher.

We invite you on a journey of a lifetime and the lifetimes of all those who come into contact with you as you teach and lead America to a greater future, a more perfect union. This book is a start for you, the teacher, and for us, the authors, on this journey. The exercises we have put into this book, the leadership theory and best practices, and the four levels of leadership we have described, will be with you every step of the way as you become a better leader.

We invite you to participate as a leader, in your school, in every organization where you participate, in your family, in your communities, on the Web, and in all outlets that serve you and serve the teaching profession that serves us all. We want you to take the initiative and not wait for others to say that it is "OK" for you to be a leader. While we think the following "letter" is nice, and was created with the best of intentions since it represents a letter of support from principals to teachers to encourage you to be better leaders, we do not think it is necessary.

We think teachers can now write their own letters of support to become better leaders. That is the key message of this book. Here is a copy of the letter created by the Lee School District of Florida in support of leadership development for teachers found on March 8, 2009 at: www.curriculum.leeschools. net/Programs/Leadership/Letter%20of%20Principal%20Support1.doc.

LETTER OF PRINCIPAL SUPPORT
LEADERSHIP DEVELOPMENT FOR TEACHERS

Please complete the top portion of this agreement **PRIOR** to teacher participation in the training.

Leadership Development for Teachers is a blended classroom and Web-based professional development course designed to meet the needs of teachers who have a desire to engage in developing their leadership knowledge and skills in order to improve student outcomes in their classrooms and schools.

I support the selection of the teacher named below as a participant in the Leadership Development for Teachers (LDT) professional development training.

_____   _____

Teacher Name   Principal Name

_____   _____

Teacher Signature   Principal Signature

The bottom portion will need to be completed prior to implementation of a school-based project.

_____

I agree to support the teacher as he/she establishes a course of action and implements the following:

*Influencing Action Plan Topic: _____

Timeline for Implementation: _____

Expected Outcome: _____

*IAP should align with classroom/department goals and /or School Improvement Plan.

_____   _____

Principal Name   Principal Signature

Next Step for Teachers

Leaders build the energy to be a leader and to become a better leader from within themselves and their support network. They do not rely on others to anoint them as leaders. Note, the leadership form above is supposed to be filled out PRIOR to taking the training. Today, you, our nation's PreK–12 teachers, have completed this book, and now you can continue your training as a leader not by asking someone else to fill out a form, but by you filling out your own training program that you deem appropriate.

A starter kit of leadership development exercises is spelled out below in Appendix A. Today, you embark on a step that will transform your lives and the lives of all you touch. Leadership development is not just for "exemplary" teachers. It is for every teacher in PreK–12 education. Leadership development is the path to becoming an exemplary teacher in an exemplary school.

We can only conclude this book with one statement:

Thank you for being our teachers and thank you for being a leader.

Appendix A

Additional Leadership Development Exercises for the Teacher

BUILDING LEADERSHIP CAPACITY—EXERCISE 6

Understanding How You Fit in the Change Cycle

The first level of leadership is described and fueled by self-awareness. Good leaders understand their talents, preferences, and personality traits. They also understand how their preferences affect others around them.

Exercise 6:

The change cycle has been described in various ways by psychologists and students of organizational change. These models usually have between four and six stages beginning with denial or loss and ending with confidence and commitment. The change cycle below has been created by combining numerous change cycle models.

Assume a major change has been directed by school administrators. A typical set of reactions that can occur among teachers is identified below.

A) At which stage of the change cycle would you place yourself initially when a change is called for by school administrators?

B) At which stage of the change cycle would you place other teachers in your school or organization?

C) After your initial reaction to the statement by school administrators to make the dramatic change, what cycle usually comes up for you, and what behaviors describe your actions in this stage in the cycle?

D) What could leaders in the organization do to help you move to "confidence" or remain at the confidence stage?

Denial

☐ Shock, apathy, focus on the past
☐ "This too will pass."
☐ "How can we stay the same?"

Resistance to Leaving the Familiar

☐ Self-doubt, blaming, anger, discord
☐ Feeling that previous efforts have been diminished or discounted

Confidence

☐ Teamwork, focus, and planning
☐ Commitment to making changes effective
☐ Feeling of accomplishment
☐ "We can do this!"

Exploration/ Management of Change

☐ "Too many ideas!"
☐ "Too much to do!"
☐ Attempts to manage change
☐ Frustration, difficulty focusing

Refocusing and Collaboration

☐ Teamwork, focus, and planning
☐ Commitment to making changes effective
☐ "I can see some things working."

E) What could you do as a teacher to help move others to confidence if you believe the change will benefit the school if all teachers get on board?

F) What could other teachers in the organization do to help the entire school move to "confidence" or remain at the confidence stage?

BUILDING LEADERSHIP CAPACITY—EXERCISE 7

Preference for Change

Exercise 7:

A) In this exercise, place yourself on the following perspectives regarding change. Please note that these positions form a continuum:

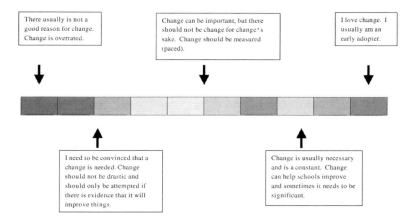

B) Do you think where you place yourself on the continuum affects where your fellow teachers would put their perspectives or attitudes regarding change? If not, why not? If so, how do you impact others' perspectives or attitudes regarding change?

C) Evaluate objectively how your perspective regarding change affects your organization's ability to bring about change?

D) What actions should school administrators undertake in order to take into account your perspective and your fellow teachers' perspective regarding change to help the change proposed be more effective?

E) What actions can you take to understand other teachers' perspectives regarding change?

F) How would understanding other teachers' perspectives regarding change help you become a better leader?

BUILDING LEADERSHIP CAPACITY—EXERCISE 8

Expanding Perspective

Perspective is one of the most fundamental qualities that separate a leader from many other employees in the school. Perspective involves understanding others' points of view and understanding the interests of the larger organization. Perspective also allows the leader to reserve judgment when faced with partial information or information that does not seem accurate.

Exercise 8:

A) Consider the following scenario from the perspective of a parent, teacher, principal, and central office administrator, respectively.

Two sixth-grade students, Billy and Jack, got into a fist-fight during lunch. Only a few punches were thrown and neither student suffered any significant physical harm. The teacher on duty wrote the office referral. The assistant principal investigated and recommended that Billy receive a 5-day suspension and Jack a 10-day suspension. Jack's mother says she will "sue the school" if her son is suspended for more than 5 days.

B) Which person(s) or group is likely to have the following information (put the number of the specific information in the appropriate box or boxes):

Table A.1

Parent	Teacher	Principal	Central Office

1. Details about what actually happened between the two boys
2. Knowledge about factors at home that are affecting Jack's behavior
3. Information about other disciplinary incidents involving either Billy or Jack
4. Knowledge of Colorado law regarding suspensions and expulsions
5. Information from student witnesses concerning the incident
6. Knowledge of the academic proficiency of both students
7. Knowledge of the school's discipline plan and policies
8. Knowledge of Jack's behavior in 5th grade
9. Concern of other parents regarding Jack's behavior
10. Information about how Jack's dad treats him
11. Billy's motivation for getting into this particular fight
12. Jack's motivation for getting into this particular fight
13. The influence of Jack's siblings on his behavior
14. Knowledge of the school's decision in similar cases
15. Knowledge of District policy with regard to student discipline
16. School trends with regard to bullying
17. Disabilities of either student (including IEPs and 504s)
18. Knowledge of how Billy's or Jack's behavior affects other students
19. School Board philosophy with regard to student discipline
20. Concerns in the community regarding student discipline

C) Which person(s) or group has an interest in the following (put the number of the specific interest in the appropriate box or boxes):

Table A.2

Parent	Teacher	Principal	Central Office

1. Jack missing as few days of school as possible
2. The safety of all the students in the school
3. Reinforcing the antibullying program in the school
4. Following school board policy
5. Following school policy
6. Keeping Jack safe at school
7. Keeping Jack safe at home
8. Keeping Billy safe at school
9. Maintaining safe schools throughout the community
10. Maintaining the perception of safe schools among the larger community
11. Building community support for school and district programs
12. Engaging parents
13. Supporting teachers and staff with student discipline issues
14. Showing Jack he is cared for
15. Improving Jack's academic achievement

D) Of the information items listed above, which are essential for a person to have before making a decision on suspending Jack or before making a judgment about the decision?

E) Of the interests listed above, which five are the ones that you would consider most in making a decision on suspending Jack or taking other action?

BUILDING LEADERSHIP CAPACITY—EXERCISE 9

Making Sense of New Information

Level two leaders actively and attentively listen and seek to understand. When faced with partial information, they reserve judgment. They first try to make sense of new concepts and ideas and help others make sense of them.

Exercise 9:

A) Imagine you hear one of the following statements while at the drinking fountain:

- "All teachers and support staff will have to be trained in either CPR or administering emergency first aid."
- "The Superintendent is going to decrease the number of student-teacher contact days by a full week."
- "Students are out of control! Most of them have over 10 unexcused absences this semester already and most of them have been referred to the office three times!"
- "The State Legislature is going to set the window for the start and end of the school year, and school will not start before the 25th of August."
- "Since the District didn't pass the mill levy override, teacher positions will be cut drastically and class sizes will go up to 30 students."
- "Now we have to administer two SCRs (paragraphs) a month. Where are we going to find the time?"

B) How do you make sense of this information for yourself and for others?

- Are you getting accurate information or only part of the picture?
- Do you understand the information? What is the context?
- What clarification or additional information do you still need to make an informed judgment?
- Whose perspective and what interests should you consider while formulating your own reaction and before relaying the information as presented?
- In what ways can you explain the rationale for the change, action, requirement, etc.?

C) How might you build perspective—an appreciation for the bigger picture or the interests of other individuals, groups, or organizations?

BUILDING LEADERSHIP CAPACITY—EXERCISE 10

Expanding Perspective

Perspective is one of the most fundamental qualities that separate a leader from many other employees in the school. Perspective involves understanding others' points of view and understanding the interests of the larger organization. Perspective also allows the leader to reserve judgment when faced with partial information or information that does not seem accurate.

Exercise 10:

A) Read the following two versions of a possible conversation between two teachers, Brenda and Tammy.

Version One

Brenda (4th grade team leader): "I heard the Curriculum Director is coming by today to observe instruction."

Tammy (colleague): "Why is she doing that?"

Brenda: "I don't know; I guess she wants to 'check up' on us."

Tammy: "I'm so tired of the mistrust. Why can't they just leave us alone to teach?"

Brenda: "Yeah, I know. Teaching's not fun any more. Anyway, you'd better put up a lesson objective just to be safe."

Tammy: "You see – just more work!" (closing the door to her classroom)

Version Two

Brenda: "The Curriculum Director may be coming by today to observe instruction."

Tammy: "Why is she doing that?"

Brenda: "I'm not sure, but she may want to observe how curriculum alignment is going."

Tammy: "I'm so tired of the mistrust. Why can't they just leave us alone to teach?"

Brenda: "It sounds like you are frustrated with some of the observations. From her perspective, though, she is providing some feedback to the principal on one of the things this district values most—the quality of the instruction. Don't you find some of the feedback to be useful?"

Tammy: "Sometimes. But now I have to put up lesson objectives."

Brenda: "Hey, as a team, we're making good progress on those and on engaging students. I'll bet she notices."

B) Describe how does Brenda demonstrate level two leadership in Version Two?

BUILDING LEADERSHIP CAPACITY—EXERCISE 11

Understanding Goals and Priorities

Level two leaders understand the goals and priorities of the organization. They understand their role in the organization and understand the role others play in serving the organization.

Exercise 11:

- As far as you know, what are the top three priorities of your school this year?
- From your perspective, what should be the top three priorities of the school?

- Review your answers to the two questions above. Rate the level of congruence between the two sets of answers.
- Great congruence
  - Mostly congruent
  - Somewhat congruent
  - Not very congruent
  - Definitely not congruent
- What steps could the school's administrators take to help get greater congruence between the two sets of answers?
- What actions could you take to develop greater congruence between the two sets of answers?

ADDITIONAL EXERCISES

Adapted from: *Learning to Lead: A Workbook On Becoming A Leader.* Bennis, Warren and Goldsmith, Joan, (Reading, MA. Addison Wesley, 1994).

In this section, we provide suggestions for activities that can be done very quickly by people who want to improve their leadership skills and aptitude. It is best to spend time on those that interest you and, if you like, write down your answers in a "leadership notebook."

1. Identify five goals you have for the next twelve months.
2. Identify five successful leaders you have known in your life and by each name write two or three key behaviors, attitudes, philosophies, or habits that helped them be successful leaders.
3. Write down five or more occasions in chronological order when you believe you were a successful leader and by each occasion explain why you think you chose to be a leader at that time and what made you successful as a leader on that occasion.
4. Describe five or more occasions where you helped someone else be a successful leader.
5. Describe five or more occasions where you have helped a student become a leader.
6. Describe five or more occasions when you saw that a change was needed in an organization where you were a teacher or were a member and you *took* an active role in seeing to it that the desired change actually took place? Why did you take an active role?
7. Describe five or more occasions when you saw that a change was needed in an organization where you worked or were a member and you *did not*

take an active role in seeing to it that the desired change actually took place? Describe why did you not take an active role?

8. Describe what you believe to be all of the costs or risks of taking on a leadership role.

9. Describe what you believe to be all of the benefits of taking on a leadership role.

10. Describe your own process of weighing the costs and risks of taking on a leadership role versus the benefits.

11. Do you believe that being a leader takes more time than being a follower? And, if so, is this one of the major reasons why you do not lead more often or seek leadership positions?

12. As a teacher, describe five ways that being a more effective leader might actually reduce the amount of time you spend doing certain activities.

13. Describe five examples where either you or another teacher improved the behavior and discipline in a class or school through an act of leadership.

14. As a teacher, describe five ways you would like to be a better leader.

15. If you do not believe that teachers should be leaders, please describe why not.

16. Form a group of five teachers and meet every other week or once a month for a couple of hours after school to discuss how over the past two weeks or month, each of you acted as leaders. You may want to call this group your leadership circle and every once in a while all of the leadership circles of your school (say two to three times a year) could meet for two hours and bring in an outside speaker or have teachers in your school report on progress they have made and challenges they have faced in their efforts to be better leaders. You will want someone to write up the "best practices" or "lessons learned" from your leadership circles meetings and share them with other teachers.

17. Make a list of what you have read on leadership development and then make a list of things you might like to read on leadership development over the next year.

18. Create a "list-serve" or email list of all of the teachers at your school to discuss leadership ideas, practices, challenges and opportunities.

19. One of the key jobs of a leader is to help others set goals and inspire them to achieve them. Describe five ways you have done this recently with your students.

20. Leaders communicate precisely, effectively, and without embarrassment. Rate yourself (1 is poor and 10 is great) on your current ability to communicate in this manner and revisit your rating each month and re-rate yourself. Write down at least once each month a situation where you communicated at an 8, 9, or 10 level.

Appendix A

A GUIDELINE TO FORMING A PEER
GROUP OR BUDDY SYSTEM

We hope you will implement our suggestion to create a peer group of teachers who meet regularly to discuss leadership and to give each other feedback regarding each person in the group's leadership approaches. Should you decide to do this, the following list of topics represent just some of the topics your group can discuss in any order. For all topics discussed in your group, we recommend that someone take notes and share them with the group right after the meeting. These notes will help form your own leadership development workbook and will be very useful as a reference on leadership topics such as:

1. Five good approaches to becoming a better leader
2. Ways to become a better teacher through being a better leader
3. Exploring how being a better leader could help teachers have a more satisfying experience teaching
4. Five ways becoming a better leader could help students improve their educational outcomes and make their educational experience more satisfying
5. Identifying best practices to becoming better at setting goals and achieving them
6. Identifying ways to use my time more efficiently and effectively
7. Identify ways to learn how to delegate more effectively
8. How to improve my communication style to be more effective
9. Learn how to calculate risk more accurately and be willing to take reasonable risks
10. Identify ways to understand people better so you can predict how people will react to your leadership actions
11. Identify ways to write, distribute and publish articles to your point of view known by others
12. Find ways to identify and eliminate bad habits
13. Find ways to set new standards for yourself and others
14. Learn how to plan farther ahead on projects and in your own life
15. Learn how to assess your own performance accurately
16. Learn how to improve the performance of others
17. Learn how to and be willing to set bigger and better goals for myself
18. Learn how to help others set bigger and better goals for themselves
19. Identify effective ways to take on more responsibility for improving other teachers
20. Identify effective ways to take on more responsibility for improving my school

21. Learn how to take on more responsibility for improving teacher and student retention
22. Identify five ways to improve communication and interactions with students' parents
23. Learn how to help parents improve their positive influence on their children
24. Learn how to help parents improve their ability to help their children with school work
25. Learn how to help students visualize their full potential
26. Identify ways to improve extracurricular activities at my school
27. Learn how to provide constructive criticism to others that promotes improvement without generating resentment
28. Learn how to form groups and get fellow teachers to support my ideas for school improvement
29. Improve my ability to inform leaders that they are not pursuing a track that will be successful
30. Improve my ability to hold leaders accountable for their actions
31. Improve my ability to spot and communicate solutions to problems
32. Improve my ability to maintain my enthusiasm and the motivation of others around me
33. Improve my ability to recognize early signs of burn out and take corrective, restorative action
34. Learn how to effectively challenge rules and actions in my school that inappropriately obstruct or inhibit success
35. Identify five ways to acknowledge others for valued behavior or for being leaders
36. Learn how to deal with fear, nervousness, or being scared so it does not impede your ability to take effective action
37. Learn how to help others act and lead successfully when they are fearful, nervous or scared
38. Identify ways to anticipate (and deal with) challenges I will face when I embark on a project where I am a leader
39. Learn how to establish roles for others whom I will lead in a team format
40. Identify cost-effective ways to reward others for their efforts
41. Learn how to motivate others
42. Identify ways to become a better, more active listener
43. Identify ways to become better at getting to the bottom of things, the facts
44. Learn how to visualize success
45. Learn how to help others visualize success
46. Learn how to set achievable goals
47. Learn how to help others set achievable goals
48. Identify ways to help students break habits that contribute to their failure

49. Identify ways to manage conversations without dominating them
50. Learn how to set excellent agendas for meetings
51. Learn how to mediate and resolve conflicts among people or groups
52. Learn how not to fear superiors
53. Learn how to treat subordinates fairly
54. Learn how to maximize the performance of all team members
55. Learn how to maximize my performance
56. Develop ideas and strategies that will help you to create significant meaning in my projects and goals
57. Learn how to help others create meaning to their projects and goals
58. Learn how to create an environment to help promote success
59. Learn how to tell hard truths when telling the truth is very hard
60. Learn how to call others on lack of integrity
61. Learn how to demand high ethical standards of myself and everyone else
62. Learn how to prioritize my projects and discard low priority projects

The discussions on each of these topics can take minutes or hours and will yield key insights as teachers get together and focus on developing their role as leaders.

Appendix B

Defining the Brands of Leadership

We define approximately 90 brands of leadership that are currently on the market. We have divided them into the following sixteen categories.

1. Ethical Leadership
2. Bad/Dysfunctional Leadership
3. Single-Leader Focus
4. Interactive Focus
5. Follower Focus
6. Multileader Focus
7. New Challenge Orientation
8. Nontraditional Organization
9. Results Orientation
10. Leadership Development/Training
11. Situational Leadership
12. Team Orientation Leadership
13. Traditional Leadership Brands
14. Visionary Leadership
15. Holistic Follower Orientation
16. Holistic Leader Orientation

We believe these categories accurately describe and categorize the types of leadership brands being taught today.

CATEGORY 1
ETHICAL LEADERSHIP

Character-based leadership: Character-based leaders place the common good at the core of their goals, and their leadership demonstrates concern for the personal development of their followers. Successful character-based leadership improves productivity and decreases worker turnover, because followers sense that they are assets and not expenses. In turn, this improves customer service and the quality of products overall. This leadership style or brand combines principle-centered leadership and servant leadership in a way that combines principle-centered leadership's integrity with the servant leadership's foundational goal of helping others.

Conscious leadership: John Renesch, author of numerous books on business, coined the term "conscious leadership" to describe leadership that originates from an individual's inner moral sense. According to Renesch, the conscious leader intuitively knows right from wrong and leads from a moral compass instead of from a prescribed code. Such leaders are likely to spontaneously take the lead when they sense a leadership vacuum, regardless of their official position. Conscious leadership radiates outward from the individual and seeks to take into account the group consciousness of all people involved in a project.

Contributory leadership: This term denotes leaders whose purpose and actions are designed almost exclusively to contribute to an improvement of an organization, the members of the organization, and the society at large. Contributory leadership promotes the sharing of leadership tasks and decisions quite broadly.

Ethical leadership: This brand of leadership, through the work of Jo Ann Ciulla, Ph.D., professor of leadership at the Jepson School of Leadership of the University of Richmond, and others may someday develop into a full-blown theory of leadership. Ethical leadership is leadership that is guided by and accepts ethical constraints and does not accept the theory that the goal of leadership is to accomplish a result regardless of the means used to achieve the desired result.

Inspired leadership: This brand of leadership focuses on individually based, ethical leadership. Jamie Walters of Ivy Sea claims, "This very notion of inspired leadership obviously carries with it a self-referencing connection to ethics, integrity, compassion, dignity, and other 'heart-centered' and Spirit-derived reference points."

Servant leadership: The term "servant leader" was coined by Robert Green-leaf in his book, *Servant Leadership.* He describes servant leaders as those who begin with the desire to serve and then gradually develop the aspiration to lead others. Greenleaf contrasts servant leadership with his understanding that some people want to lead first, and only serve others as an ancillary objective. Thus, a spectrum exists where servant leaders and narcissistic leaders are two extremes.

Ultimately, the difference in these two brands or types of leaders is whether the leader is more concerned with personal recognition and ego or with the personal growth and well-being of his or her followers and the community the leader serves. Servant leaders are inclusive, and want to serve their community and use their leadership skills and position to expand the leadership roles and capacities of those they serve. Often servant leaders do not hold formal leadership position but lead with influence and encourage collaboration among their followers. Servant leaders emphasize and demonstrate how ethics is an integral part of leadership through the example they set for others.

Steward leadership: Peter Block and Katherine Tyler Scott, president, Trustee Leadership Development, have written several influential books on this brand of leadership. This brand of leadership says that leaders are responsible for making decisions about and managing the resources over which the leader has control or influence. Steward leaders manage these resources ethically and solely in the interest of the people whose resource the leader is designated to manage.

In the corporate world, steward leadership includes being a good leader of people, a good steward of products and services, and a leader of the community. It maintains that the power to lead originates from below and is exclusively for the benefit of others. This type of leadership also has strong religious connotations and specifically rejects exploiting power and leadership opportunities for the benefit of the leader.

Trustee leadership: This brand of leadership popularized by Katherine Tyler Scott and others is directed to boards of directors and describes how leaders balance the relationship between their self-interest and the good of their followers and community. Trustee leaders believe that their role as leaders is completely tied to the common good, and they try to integrate the personal aspects of being a leader with professional, individual, and community interests that grow out of their leadership actions.

Trustee leadership can apply in the for-profit, nonprofit, political, and policy realms. James Kouzes, author of *The Leadership Challenges,* writes that "you cannot lead others until you have first led yourself through a struggle of opposing values." Trustee leaders both develop a vision and participate as trustees of the leadership position and status that others have conferred upon them.

Values-based leadership: This brand of leadership requires the leader to understand the different and sometimes contrasting ideas, values, and needs of those involved in a project or organization and, then articulate the moral and ethical values and principles upon which the leader bases his or her decisions and actions. People from Steve Jobs, the cofounder of Apple Computer, Inc., to General Norman Schwartzkopf claim that values based leadership is most important in today's business world and in public life because people who care about similar values work best together and can build the bonds of trust required for successful leadership.

Values-based leadership encourages trust and can be very helpful when building interpersonal relationships. Values-based leadership includes three key areas, effectiveness, morality, and a focus on long-term goals.

Values-centered leadership: William J. O'Brien has written extensively about this leadership approach in his book, *The Soul of Corporate Leadership: Guidelines for Value-Centered Governance.* This brand of leadership occurs when the values of the leader and the values of the followers are fused and become one, emanating from either direction. In such an atmosphere, followers are involved and motivated to help others and to be a part of something larger than themselves. Sam Walton, founder of Wal-Mart, mastered this leadership technique.

The Wal-Mart training program teaches each trainee the personal values of the founder and subsequently the values of the corporation. Each follower is then expected to embrace these values, not only at work, but also in his or her personal life. Ideally, this type of leadership creates an environment where followers promote, demonstrate, and defend the organization's values.

CATEGORY 2
BAD/DYSFUNCTIONAL LEADERSHIP

Bogus leadership: This is opposite of conscious leadership. Bogus leadership is leadership occurs when leaders follow a narrow or scripted type of leadership that does not reflect who they are. Their insistence on following a single leadership paradigm limits their thinking, giving them fewer options and causing them to act more slowly than conscious leaders, who lead from their moral compass and group consciousness.

Narcissistic leadership: This type of leadership occurs when leaders are motivated primarily by their desire to serve their egos. Generally, narcissistic leaders keep very high profiles. It should be clear that narcissistic leadership does not necessarily mean unproductive leadership. Michael Maccoby, author of *The Productive Narcissist: The Promise and Peril of Visionary Leaders,* argues that narcissistic leaders are generally useful in times of transition or turbulence because they have the personal popularity and charisma to make massive changes.

Over time, however, these leaders tend to become unrealistic dreamers, and their leadership styles can drag down their companies. Narcissistic leaders tend to ignore advice and take a top-down approach to leading. Narcissistic leaders are marked by great vision and many followers, who are often more personally loyal to the narcissistic leader than to his or her vision and policies. The weaknesses of narcissistic leaders include over-sensitivity to criticism, lack of empathy, poor listening skills, distaste for mentoring, and an excessive desire to compete.

Reactive leadership: This leadership style or brand is the opposite of proactive leadership. Reactive leaders expect and assume the worst from their followers, sometimes treating them as if they were children. Reactive leaders tend to focus on weaknesses and negatives, rarely providing positive encouragement. Reactive leaders address issues only after they occur, instead of anticipating and handling future challenges. This creates an air of crisis, making the leader seem disorganized. To further complicate matters, reactive leaders are often unclear about their goals and lack a vision for the future. Because of these attributes, reactive leaders tend to punish employees after the fact rather than guide them toward a clear goal in advance.

Toxic leadership: This leadership style is also called "destructive leadership." It has been studied by Jean Lipman-Blumen in her book, *The Allure of Toxic Leaders: Why We Follow Destructive Bosses.* This brand of leadership harms an organization by focusing relentlessly on short-term goals. Toxic leadership ignores the morale of followers and their working conditions. Ultimately, toxic leaders can be identified by the long-term effects of their destructive behavior.

Their followers perform poorly for several reasons. First, they often feel compelled to over focus on the short run. Second, they are discouraged by the myopic focus on the bottom line and the poor choices inherent in their leadership style. Third, toxic leaders have poor interpersonal skills, which hurt the self-esteem of their followers, adversely affecting the entire working environment. Fourth, toxic leaders value being in control, and they will often go to great lengths in order to preserve their leadership position.

CATEGORY 3
SINGLE LEADER FOCUS

Alpha male leadership: This brand of leadership, discussed at length by Arnold M. Ludwig in his book, *King of the Mountain,* suggests that human beings, like apes and wolves, are hardwired and instinctively driven to have a dominant male be a leader of a social group. Often this leadership brand assigns great weight to physical characteristics as leading predictors of who will emerge as the leader and dominant person in the group. This brand of leadership is gender oriented in a way that is rejected by many people today. But Ludwig suggests that this brand of leadership is displayed in many of the 1,941 heads of nations during the twentieth century.

Assigned leadership: This brand refers to leadership based on positions or titles. It is similar to hereditary leadership except that, instead of attaining a leadership position through death (usually of a father), an assigned leader is appointed based on heredity, merit, or other factors. It is very popular in the military. In some cases, assigned leaders are insecure in their positions because they have no popular base. This insecurity often manifests itself as authoritarian, and sometimes even dictatorial, leadership. Accountability is often important to counteract some of the potential negative behavior associated with this type of leadership.

Authentic leadership: This brand advocated by Kevin Cashman, author of *Leadership from the Inside Out,* defines authentic leadership as the leadership that radiates from the core of a person. He states, "leadership is authentic self-expression that creates value." Cashman defines five key areas of authentic leadership: (1) knowing oneself authentically, (2) listening authentically, (3) expressing one's self authentically, (4) appreciating authentically, and (5) serving authentically.

In order to be an authentic leader, a person must serve first and lead second. Authentic leaders seek to set an example for all of their followers and for other leaders through their actions and how they approach their leadership responsibilities.

Leadership by example: This brand is adopted by leaders who seek to use their own actions as a guide to their followers. In short, leadership by example implies that leaders should do everything with the same ethical and quality standards that they require of others. There are two parts to this type of leadership: (1) doing what should be done in every situation and (2) doing it according to high standards of exemplary behavior. Leadership by example can have the positive effect of inspiring followers to have the same goals and commitment as leaders and to adopt their methods and approaches to leadership tasks.

Charismatic leadership: This brand of leadership, discussed in the 1800s by Max Weber and many others, is distinguished from other types of leadership because charismatic leaders inspire people to follow them. Charismatic leaders impress their own visions and goals upon their followers and make their followers see things the way they do. Charismatic leaders radiate self-confidence, fearlessly lead, and know how to communicate their positions and ideas without embarrassment or reservation.

Followers often turn to charismatic leaders during times of organizational, corporate, or social turmoil. Charismatic leadership tends to follow the traditional or heroic leadership model. Charismatic leaders lead from the top down and followers generally do not participate in the decision-making process. One great danger of this brand of leadership is that followers can become blind to what the leader is actually doing and never question the results the leader is actually trying to achieve.

Directive leadership: This brand of leadership is the opposite of participative leadership. In times of crisis, people tend to turn to directive leaders, because directive leadership points the way to safety. Directive leaders take charge, make decisions, and expect their decisions to be implemented without question. They are willing to revise goals and provide solutions unilaterally, using the traditional top-down approaches to leading. When the difficult times are past, followers often prefer leaders who are less directive, instead favoring those who seek input before making decisions. Modern history provides numerous examples of directive leadership.

For example, democracies tend to reelect directive leaders during times of war. Wartime presidents tend to be more decisive and unilateral than others, and people accept and welcome these traits in times of war or crisis. When the crisis passes, however, the heavy-handed, dictatorial methods of some directive leaders often become unpopular with the voting public. This type of leadership is often replaced by a leader who is more participatory, collaborative, and consultative.

Integrated leadership: This brand of leadership was popularized by Ken Rafferty of Executive Consulting, who argues that integrated leadership involves all aspects of the human condition and creates new ways to get people involved in what they are doing, He says that integrated leadership helps executives understand the power and usefulness of embracing values, trust, participation, learning, creating, and sharing within the work environment.

It also involves connecting the various people and departments in an organization with one another to achieve a common purpose decided upon by an organization through involving all of the members of the organization in setting the tone and direction for the organization.

Leaders building leaders: This brand or model of leadership has been promoted by Peter Drucker, Jack Welch, and many others. The basic tenet of this brand of leadership is that the primary purpose of a leader is to build up the capabilities of followers so that one can step in and take over should a leader, for any reason, not be able or willing to lead further. The key is that in order for a company to maintain success, the current leaders must continually prepare future leaders.

Leaders building leaders is a results-based leadership strategy that promotes future leaders by encouraging "upward" or "trickle-up" leadership and by using 360-degree feedback and other leadership assessment tools. The leaders building leaders brand helps organizations increase their leadership resources, eases transitions, and increases stability.

Leadership at every step: This brand of leadership suggests that leadership is a full-time, 24/7 job and is a lifelong process instead of something that one can do on occasion or as an isolated act during a lifetime. It is an approach used by organizations that believe that leadership can and should occur in every part of an organization and at all times. Leadership at every step implies that all people can lead and have a responsibility to do so.

Postmortem leadership: This brand of leadership describes the influence strong, heroic leaders can have on their successors and organizations after they leave. This type of leadership can have a profound impact on policy and decision making in the future of many organizations. Postmortem leadership occurs when current leaders try to govern using the formulas and ideas of their predecessor(s) instead of creating their own or following the desires of their followers as they evolve.

Supportive leadership: In *Art of Supportive Leadership,* J. Donald Walters argues a supportive leader always recognizes that people are very important and not just tools for the leaders to use. Supportive leaders are loyal to and supportive of their followers. The classic example of this type of leadership is the general who stays at the front with his troops, despite the dangers to himself. Supportive leaders emphasize having high levels of confidence in and improving the competence in their followers. Supportive leaders are not micromanagers and give their followers substantial room to contribute to leadership decisions and to exhibit leadership behaviors.

Versatile leadership: Robert Kaiser and Robert Kaplan state that versatile leadership consists of a synthesis between balanced leadership and strategic leadership. The versatile leader must balance of leadership traits and approaches at each moment. This type of leadership is dynamic and situationally determined.

CATEGORY 4
INTERACTIVE FOCUS

Achievement-oriented leadership: This brand of leadership is one aspect of Robert House's path-goal theory discussed in the text of this book. This type of leader sets high goals and difficult challenges for both the leader and the team. This type of leader also provides encouragement for the members and expresses confidence in the ability of the group to complete the assigned task. Achievement-oriented leaders are ultimately interested results, but their leadership focuses on more than just the bottom line. By motivating followers, by challenging them, and by giving positive feedback, this leader can promote improved productivity.

Appreciative leadership: This brand of leadership teaches leaders to look for and find the best in people and acknowledge people for the good things they do. It is designed to help facilitate communication between leaders and followers, because the leader actively seeks out input from those below him or her. It makes a working environment friendlier by focusing on the positives instead of the negatives. The central idea behind appreciative leadership and its related field called "appreciative inquiry" is that the leader shows the followers that they are appreciated, and he or she tries to work with their strengths whenever possible in order to inspire passion and build self-confidence among them.

Functional leadership or function-centered leadership: This concept, pioneered by Elisabeth Cox and Cynthia House, means that leadership is function centered rather than person centered.[1] Leadership is viewed as encompassing critical things to be done, rather than as the characteristics of one person. Function-centered leadership requires that all persons practice leadership by leading in those areas where they have critical responsibilities.

---

1   Elisabeth Cox and Cynthia House, "Functional Leadership: A Model for the Twenty-First Century" in *Building Leadership Bridges* 2001 (University of Maryland, College Park, MD: International Leadership Association).

Leadership as a process: This brand of leadership makes the distinction between leadership as a solitary act and leadership as a function of the inter-action of leaders and followers. Peter Northouse defines leadership as a pro-cess during which an individual influences a group of individuals to achieve a common goal.[2] The philosophy behind this brand of leadership views leader-ship as something that must continually evolve. Leadership is seen as a career or lifelong path. Leadership as a process is a collaborative effort between leaders and followers. It shapes the goals of a group, motivates their behavior towards their attainment of these goals, and defines the culture of the group.

Inclusive leadership: This brand of leadership identifies the fostering of a broad range of interpersonal relationships by the leader as the single most important factor in effective leadership. Inclusive leaders are especially con-cerned with relationships between them and their followers, customers, inves-tors, suppliers, and the community. They believe that their relationships will lead to sustained growth and development within organizations because they respect their followers and focus on something other than the bottom line. Inclusive leaders act as stewards for their organizations' resources and are will-ing to share their leadership roles with others. Inclusive leadership views an organization as a network of interpersonal, mutually dependent relationships.

Inclusive leaders seek to maximize the potential of the networks. This creates a synergistic effect, because the network, when united in quest of a common goal, produces an even more powerful network. Inclusive leadership is very similar to collaborative, consultative, participatory, and servant leader-ship in emphasis and practice.

Proactive leadership: This brand of leadership is based on the belief that leaders look toward the future and make leadership decisions based on their anticipation of two things: what is going to happen in the future, and how their followers are going to react to their ideas, suggestions, decisions, and actions of leadership. This type of leadership requires leaders to understand the future and be able to connect psychologically with their followers. Proactive leaders give feedback and seek 360-degree feedback from those around them. They act decisively and clearly communicate the goals to their followers.

Self-organizing leadership/self-directed teams: Dr. Tomas Hench of the University of Wisconsin, Madison, defines "self-organizing leadership" as "a

---

2 Peter Northouse, *Leadership: Theory and Practice: Sage Reflections*, 3rd ed., (Sage: Thousand Oaks, CA, 2004).

quality that manifests itself as a relationship between the leader and the led; in the context of a particular challenge, facing a particular group of people, in a particular moment of time." Thus, self-organizing leadership spontaneously manifests itself at any level of an organization in order to meet current challenges. Often, these are communication challenges between and among departments or employees in an organization.

Using self-organizing leadership can add significant value to an organization because it helps to capitalize on latent abilities of each member. It also tends to improve work patterns and processes because people concentrate on building their own future and lessens resistance to change, because the people themselves are generating and leading the change.

CATEGORY 5
FOLLOWER FOCUS

Collaborative leadership: John Gardner, author of *On Leadership,* defines this brand of leadership as one in which leaders seek the strong input of followers in assisting them in making decisions and leading the group. This brand also requires the followers to join together and offer their time, assets, and commitment to help formulate key decisions that will address the most difficult issues facing a group. According to John Gardner, collaborative leaders inspire commitment and action by creating visions and working with their followers to solve problems.

Collaborative leaders lead, not from the top down, but as peer problem solvers who help others without autocratically making decisions. They take responsibility for building extensive community and member involvement and for sustaining hope and participation from their followers. They seek input from all involved parties. They help to keep the group on track by setting realistic, concrete goals and by rewarding the attainment of these goals with positive reinforcement. Collaborative leadership looks at the big picture and at long-term goals and considers the global, complex, and systematic nature of problems.

Consultative leadership: This brand of leadership includes building strong relationships and relies on these relationships for organizations to expand and meet challenges. Consultative leadership allows for the strong participation of followers in the decision-making process. It must be flexible and capable of extending across the leadership-followership border, and actually blurring this border. It is designed to deal effectively with problems that neither are clearly defined, nor have obvious solutions. Ron Heifetz refers to these kinds of problems as "adaptive problems."

Empowering leadership: This leadership brand is discussed by Peter Block in his book, *The Empowered Manager* and is very similar to participatory leadership in which the leader delegates authority to followers, empowering them to make decisions, and giving them a direct stake in bringing about change. Theoretically, this reduces the resistance to change and increases the morale of the followers, causing them to work harder, because they are directly involved in leading their organizations.

Entrepreneurial leadership: This brand of leadership instills followers with the confidence to think, behave, and act as entrepreneurs in the interest of their organization. An entrepreneurial leader focuses on encouraging every follower to help create economic value through the deployment of limited resources.

Organizational leadership: This style of leadership, popularized by Theodore White's book *Organizational Man,* stresses allegiance to an organization. It seeks to capitalize on people's desire to be a part of something larger than themselves and urges people to identify themselves as a part of the organization.

Participative leadership: Participative leadership is a type of leadership in which leaders involve others in the decision-making process. Participative leadership is based on the idea that in order to be effective, participative leaders need to encourage their followers to make suggestions and lead the implementation of these suggestions.

Upward/trickle-up leadership/upside-down leadership: Michael Useem, professor at the Wharton School and author of *Leading Up: How to Lead Your Boss So You Both Win,* and Tom Chappell, *Managing Upside Down: Seven Intentions of Value-Centered Leadership,* define upward leadership and trickle-up leadership in which followers are expected to contribute ideas and help make decisions critical to the future of the organization. Leadership, under this definition, originates from the bottom of the corporate pyramid instead of from the higher managerial ranks.

CATEGORY 6
MULTILEADER FOCUS

Distributive leadership: This brand of leadership was made popular by Richard Elmore, professor of educational leadership at Harvard. Distributive leadership stresses the sharing of leadership responsibilities among several people. Distributive leadership is also known as shared leadership, dispersed leadership, fluid leadership, collective leadership, and roving leadership.

Formative leadership: This brand developed by Dr. Ruth Ash and Dr. Maurice Persall from Samford University is based upon the idea that many different leaders should work together within a single organization. Law firms often use this type of leadership through management or executive committees. A formative leader must freely share data, information, and knowledge with a team and also facilitate knowledge transfer within the organization to promote wide distribution of leadership tasks throughout the organization.

CATEGORY 7
NEW CHALLENGES LEADERSHIP

Connective leadership: This brand of leadership, made popular by Jean Lipman-Blumen's book, *Connective Leadership: Managing in a Changing World,* takes place when leaders reach across borders (corporate, geographical, and cultural) in order to assist in building communication networks between disparate groups with conflicting needs and goals.

Creative leadership: According to Lyndon Rego from the Center for Creative Leadership, creative leaders seek to create the future in a conscious manner by anticipating and responding creatively to new situations.

Cross-border leadership: This brand of leadership refers to leadership that transcends geographic, cultural, and corporate borders in order to accomplish a given task. It requires excellent communication skills, because the involved parties often have different (if not conflicting) ideas, expectations, and goals. As the world continues to get smaller, or flatter as Thomas Friedman suggests, cross-border leadership will become increasingly important.

CATEGORY 8
NONTRADITIONAL ORGANIZATIONS

Chaordic leadership: This brand of leadership was popularized by Dee Hock, Founder and CEO Emeritus of Visa International, Inc. He coined the term to describe leadership that is both chaotic and orderly. Chaordic leadership differentiates between the relationship between superiors/subordinates and leaders/followers. The former relationship relies upon the coercive power of the supervisor, whereas the latter is a matter of choice for the follower.

Chaordic leadership consists of four behaviors, the first three of which should occupy approximately 95 percent of a leader's time: (1) managing one's own character, (2) managing one's peers, (3) managing one's superiors, and (4) managing those below. In this brand of leadership, Dee Hock defies many ethical leadership theorists by proposing that the duty for ensuring ethical leadership lies within the power of the followers.

Complexity leadership: This brand of leadership, like quantum leadership, draws on the idea that Newtonian physics is not very applicable to the modern business climate, law firms, corporations, or nonprofit organizations. Complexity leadership encourages spontaneous self-organization and unplanned but sensible improvements in the efficacy of organizations.

Complexity leaders do not lead from the top down, but rather expect that their followers will form networks and find ways to lead themselves. This means that goals and production strategies are always being streamlined and ensures that new ideas circulate freely in the organization that adopts the principles of complexity leadership.

Consultative leadership: This brand of leadership is based upon the belief that many of today's challenges are bigger and more complex than the abilities of any single leader to solve them. Consultative leaders thus focus on listening, participation, and facilitating a dialogue between themselves and their followers. When this is done properly, it has a synergistic effect for the entire team and creates better solutions than can be created through a command and control or top-down traditional leadership formula. Consultative leadership puts the leader in a role closer to the traditional role of a moderator or facilitator.

Quantum leadership: This brand of leadership borrows its conceptual base from quantum physics and was made popular by Tim Porter-O'Grady's book, *Quantum Leadership: A Textbook of New Leadership.* Although Newtonian physics is dominated by highly structured interactions between objects, quantum theory holds that these interactions are chaotic and unpredictable. Quantum leadership brings this distinction to the world of business and organizational development. Newtonian organizations have the traditional pyramid organizational structure. In Newtonian structures, those on top, the leaders, are expected to control the followers—treating them as tools rather than creative assets.

The bureaucratic framework in Newtonian structures is rigid and includes multiple layers of approval required when a person at the bottom of the pyramid makes a suggestion for change or attempts in any way to act as a leader. Newtonian organizations find it difficult to adjust their direction, to innovate, experiment, or adapt in the changing world.

A quantum organization, on the other hand, is one in which all members design and manage the organization's systems and processes. Information flows freely from one area of the organization to the other, not just from the top down. Quantum leadership is based on the idea that anyone within an organization can lead and should develop leadership skills. Quantum leaders help people develop self-managing strategies. Ideally, they teach that organizations are as much about growth and development of the individual members or parts as they are about creating products and delivering services.

CATEGORY 9
RESULTS ORIENTED LEADERSHIP

Results-based leadership: This brand of leadership was popularized by Dave Ulrich, Jack Zenger, and Norman Smallwood in their book, *Results-Based Leadership.* They explain that results-based leadership places a relentless emphasis on outcomes through the following equation: effective leadership = results. In order to measure a leader's ability or aptitude, one must look to results as the best measure.

Results-based leadership focuses on four areas of results: (1) employee results (i.e., productivity), (2) organizational results, (3) customer oriented results, and (4) profits or returns—investor results.

Scientific leadership: This brand of leadership focuses on the ability to measure the effects of leader. The success or failure of a leader who follows the brand or discipline of scientific leadership is determined by how well the people under him or her perform.

CATEGORY 10
LEADERSHIP TRAINING BRANDS

Leadership development: This generic category embodies the assumption that leaders are made, not born. Leadership development programs focus on identifying new ways to teach people how to assess and improve their leadership skills. Leadership development courses tend to be based on leadership theories, whereas leadership training is more concerned with fine-tuning technical leadership skills such as speech making, project management, communication, and team-building skills.

Executive development: This aspect or brand of leadership training teaches and develops the skills that high-level managers need. Executive development programs build critical-thinking and decision-making skills necessary to anticipate and meet various challenges.

Leader to leader: This leadership brand asserts that leaders can improve significantly by learning from their peers, other leaders. According to the Leader to Leader Institute, formerly the Drucker Foundation, bringing leaders into a forum with other leaders helps to facilitate communication and idea generation across the public, private, and social sectors.

Leadership training: This leadership concept is similar to leadership development, but focuses on technical aspects of leadership such as project management, public speaking, communication, and team building.

Unnatural leadership: David L. Dotlich and Peter C. Cairo have developed the brand called unnatural leadership, which is learned—hence the name "unnatural." Unnatural leadership promotes the ideas that leaders should think creatively and challenge conventional wisdom, admit when they do not know something and ask their followers for help unnatural leadership embraces the concepts 1) there are many solutions to a given problem; 2) trust others before they earn it; 3) connect with competitors in symbiotic relationships in order to avoid having to recreate the wheel; and 4) be willing to give up some control to improve participation.

CATEGORY 11
SITUATIONAL LEADERSHIP

Issue leadership: This brand of leadership occurs when a person takes the initial step of organizing a coalition to oppose or support a given issue. The organizers and leaders of the American Civil Liberties Union (ACLU), the National Association for the Advancement of Colored People (NAACP), the Susan B. Anthony List organization, and other single-issue types of organization fall into this category. In general, issue leaders need to be able to focus deeply on one issue, possess good social skills, and excellent networking skills.

Leading change: This brand or model of leadership promoted by John P. Kotter in his book, *Leading Change and the Society for the Leadership of Change,* focuses on the intention and ability of a leader to create and execute a vision. People who lead change efforts integrate key program goals, priorities, values, and other factors in a dynamic environment where change both occurs often and is necessary in order to address a problem or situation successfully. Leading change requires the ability to balance change and continuity.

Kotter has developed an eight-stage model for implementing change: (1) establish a sense of urgency, (2) create a guiding coalition, (3) develop a vision and strategy, (4) communicate the change and vision, (5) empower a broad base of people to act, (6) generate short-term successes, (7) consolidate gains, and (8) insure that the changes and new approaches are deeply institutionalized into the culture of the organization or society. Leading change requires leaders to be able to predict and understand when followers, and even co-leaders, will resist change in organizations.

Situational leadership: This popular brand of leadership developed and promoted by Hersey and Blanchard refers to a model of leadership that adopts different styles of leading depending on the needs of the situation and the abilities of the leaders and followers in the situation. Ken Blanchard, author of the *One Minute Manager* series, and Paul Hersey developed the basic model for situational leadership during the 1960s. Situational leadership requires great skill in analyzing a given situation in order to decide which type of leadership style or behavior to use.

Tipping-point leadership: This brand of leadership, first analyzed by Malcolm Gladwell in his book, *Tipping Point,* suggests that in order for leadership behavior to be effective, leaders should exert a concentrated influence on specific areas in order to convince a critical mass of people to adopt an idea or strategy. Tipping-point leaders seek to overcome (1) cognitive hurdles that cause people to resist change, (2) resource hurdles, (3) motivational hurdles, which discourage followers, and (4) political hurdles.

CATEGORY 12
TEAM ORIENTATION LEADERSHIP

Synergistic leadership: This brand of leadership is based on the notion of having people and organizations work together to create value from the combined efforts that will be far greater than could be created by each of the parts working independently. This intangible factor results in the $1 + 1 = 3$ philosophy of synergistic leadership. Steven Covey has popularized this type of leadership as Habit #6, Synergize.

Team leadership: This brand of leadership differs from traditional top-down leadership in eight major ways. (1) Instead of one person being solely responsible for the success or failure of an objective, the responsibility is shared by a team of people. (2) Final decisions are made by a group of people and not an autocratic leader. (3) Power is decentralized, and the structure of authority is deemphasized. (4) The role of the individual is minimized, or at least deemphasized.

(5) Task-oriented functions are performed by the group as a whole and not by single leaders. (6) The team itself is responsible for its self-maintenance. (7) Socio-emotional processes and interpersonal interactions are monitored by team leaders. (8) Expressions of feelings and ideas are encouraged and addressed by the team in open meetings. This leadership model can be inefficient and complicated, as compared with the command and control model of leadership, especially in large organizations.

The expected benefits of team leadership include improving morale, increasing the competence and leadership abilities of all members of the team, and capturing the unique abilities of each member for the good of the entire organization. Team building, an essential component of team leadership, is a leadership strategy involving improving team dynamics, clarifying team goals, identifying roadblocks, overcoming obstacles, and facilitating the achievement of the final goals.

Virtual leadership: This brand of leadership is a field pioneered by NetAge CEO Jessica Lipnack, Jeff Stamps, and Lisa Kimball, CEO of Group Jazz, Inc. It asserts that teams with members in different geographical locations that are managed by a manager who is not geographically located with other team members can be very productive, at significantly less cost, than teams in which everyone is located in the same geographical area using face-to-face meetings and communication.

Virtual leadership models rely on information technology to foster and keep track of communications, and places an emphasis on creating team unity. Virtual leaders are in charge of designing the projects and holding the team together, which requires considerable communication, usually by phone, e-mail, Web conferencing, shared documents Web sites, and other collaboration software. The May 2004 edition of the *Harvard Business Review* contains a study about virtual leadership and indicates that it can work very well in today's interconnected, globalized world.

CATEGORY 13
TRADITIONAL LEADERSHIP BRANDS

Coaching or executive coaching: This brand is as old as humans themselves. It is a leadership style in which the leader seeks to help the people he or she coaches find and explore their own goals and capabilities. This type of leadership encourages two-way communication. Ideally, coaching results in the development of the followers and allows them to become more effective as leaders.

Heroic leadership: This brand of leadership is based on the "great man" theory of leadership. Heroic leaders behave as if all the responsibility is on their shoulders and put themselves on a pedestal above their followers. This results in a top-down leadership style that causes followers to become dependent on their leaders.

Institutionalized leadership: This brand of leadership was coined by Elman Service in his 1975 book, *Origins of the State and Civilization: The Process of Cultural Evolution.* Service argues that institutionalized leadership is ingrained both in the legislative foundations of a state and in the functioning of its bureaucratic apparatus. Leadership is therefore fostered by the creation of a detailed institutional framework to allocate decision-making authority.

Military leadership: This brand of leadership refers to leadership that is organized in a top-down fashion. Military leadership is often marked by a rigid hierarchical structure and a well-defined central authority. A clear definition of values and clear lines of authority must exist for this type of powerful command and control leadership to succeed because often what followers do is a direct function of what the leader says they should do. In times of crisis, military leadership can be especially useful. Followers can clearly identify who is in charge and can be comforted and directed by this. By establishing exactly how much and what type of authority leaders in each position exert, everyone in the chain of command knows his or her role.

However, this style is subject to lack of accountability, because the authority of the position and the authority of the person can be tied very closely and not easily questioned. Often the military leadership brand does not promote significant two-way, reciprocal communication between the leader and the follower.

Muscular leadership: This is a top-down leadership brand that requires strong direction from the leader and strict obedience by followers. This leadership style contrasts with more collaborative, team-oriented approaches to leadership. David Gergen's article "President Bush's Leadership"[3] and his keynote speech to the International Leadership Association in November 2003 in Seattle, Washington,[4] explain how President Bush uses this brand of leadership.

Operational leadership: This brand of leadership, very close to the definition of "management," focuses on the day-to-day challenges facing an organization. In general, this type of leadership is very different from visionary leadership, which focuses its energy on attaining long-term goals instead of short-term ones.

Powerful leadership: This brand of leadership is espoused by Ruth Sherman in *Get Them to See It Your Way, Right Away: How to Persuade Anyone of Anything.* Powerful leaders are able to retain their influence either by building themselves up in the eyes of their followers or by destroying or eliminating their opposition. It also can result in leadership by fear or resentment, lowering morale, and thereby decreasing productivity.

Rational leadership: According to Marin Clarke, of the General Management Group at the Cranfield School of Management in England, rational leadership gives priority to traditional and accepted processes of influencing people. Rational leaders tend to prefer formal, face-to-face meetings, and leadership roles are very carefully defined.

Transactional leadership: James McGregor Burns popularized this brand of leadership in his book *Leadership,* published in 1976. Transactional leadership motivates followers by appealing to their self-interest. It motivates followers through the exchange process. Modern theorists have added to Burns's model, and today there are four types of behavior that can be considered transactional leadership: (1) contingent reward—rewards are given when expectations are met; (2) passive management by exception—correction and punishment are handed out when performance standards are not reached; (3) active management by exception—leaders actively watch work quality and correct followers; and (4) laissez-faire leadership—leaders adopts a hands-off approach to leading.

---

3   David Gergen, "President Bush's Leadership," *Compass: A Journal of Leadership,* Center for Public Leadership, Harvard University (fall 2003).

4   David Gergen, "Perspectives on Leadership" (Keynote speech. International Leadership Association, Seattle, WA, November 2003).

CATEGORY 14
VISIONARY LEADERSHIP

Anticipatory Leadership: Anika Savage and Michael Sales have developed a concept called the "anticipatory leader." The anticipatory leader seeks and evaluates information about the future on a regular basis in order to inform the leaders' views on the best strategies for dealing with expected futures. The anticipatory leader integrates the information about the future into the leader's decision making today so as to promote the organization's capacity for being successful in the future. The authors postulate that anticipatory leaders also hold a deep sense of social responsibility since they are looking to preserve and promote success for long time periods in the future.

Anticipatory leaders also are whole system thinkers and look closely at the interactions that are likely to exist when change occurs. Anticipatory leaders often communicate their views of the future and seek to have their organizations take a long run view when developing strategies and programs for their organization. The work of Savage and Sales on Anticipatory Leadership can be found in the Journal, ***Strategy and Leadership,*** Volume 38, No 6, 2008, pp. 28–35, Emerald Group Publishing.

Level five (5) leadership: Jim Collins developed the concept of *Level 5 leadership* in his book *Good to Great: Why Some Companies Make the Leap . . . and Others Don't.* Collins identified five levels of leadership. Level 1 leadership is provided by very able individuals whose knowledge, experience, and work ethic enables them to lead. Level 2 introduces the concept of teamwork and synergy, stressing that teams can accomplish more than isolated individuals working on similar projects. Level 3 is the leadership demonstrated by the team leader who motivates and encourages a team to succeed. Level 4 resembles level 3 leadership, but the leader shows more energy and demands more from each team member.

Level 5 refers to the leadership given by executives who are personally humble but demand the highest level of performance from their teams. They instill standards and a vision in their followers and use this vision to motivate them. They allow their followers the freedom and responsibility to work together and make their own decisions, while keeping them encouraged and focused on the ultimate goal of the current project. The job of the level 5 leader is to determine how to best maintain high-level organizational objectives, including cash flow and profitability, and help their followers succeed with all key organizational objectives.

Level 5 leaders set an example that they expect their followers to emulate. They sacrifice their own egos in order to help their organizations and accept responsibility for poor performance. According to Collins, level 5 leadership is the most important factor in taking a company "from good to great."

Loose-tight leadership: This brand of leadership is explained in Christopher Meyer's book, *Relentless Growth: How Silicon Valley Innovation Strategies Can Work in Your Business.* Loose-tight leadership is a style designed to culti-vate new ideas on a regular basis. Meyer claims that it "alternates the creation of space for idea generation and free exploration with a deliberate tightening that selects and tests specific ideas for further investment and development."

The first stages of innovation should be "loose," and the innovation process should tighten as it progresses. Too much of either loose or tight thinking can harm growth, because looseness can prevent a company from moving forward in a single direction and tightness can strangle creativity. At the heart of this leadership style is the goal of continuous, rapid innovation.

Principle-centered leadership: This brand of leadership is best captured by an excerpt from Stephen R. Covey's book, *Principle-Centered Leadership.* He writes that "if you focus on principles, you empower everyone who understands those principles to act without constant monitoring, evaluating, correcting, or controlling." Principle-centered leadership thus revolves around a set of prin-ciples espoused by the leader and accepted by the followers, who may provide some input to the leader regarding these principles. The leader relies upon these principles as the leader's basis for the decisions the leader makes, the style of leadership the leader uses, and as the basis for leading others in its entirety.

The principles of security, guidance, wisdom, and power are often key principles that leaders use to guide organizations that adopt this brand of leadership. Principle-centered leadership is similar to the platform-based organizations discussed in this book.

Revolutionary leadership: This brand of leadership is based on the leaders' and followers' perception that significant change is needed in a given com-munity. Revolutionary leaders are willing to take tremendous risks in order to change present conditions and alter the power relationships that currently exist. A basic problem with revolutionary leaders like Pol Pot and others is they often destroy the historic, traditional way of life and all remnants of it, but do not have a coherent strategy to replace this way of life with a better life.

Strategic leadership: According to Randal Heide, onetime president of the Strategic Leadership Forum, strategic leadership compels everyone in an organization to adopt a shared set of goals and a common vision of how to achieve success. Unlike heroic leaders who use fear or personal charisma to inspire followers or results-based leaders who make decisions based only on the bottom line, strategic leaders allow the principles and goals of the organization to guide their leadership decisions and their style of leadership.

Strategic leadership ensures that even though leaders come and go, the guidelines for leadership in the organization will remain constant. Dell, Wal-Mart, and Southwest Airlines are all examples of companies that do business according to carefully conceived strategies. Their success does not depend on a specific leader as much as it depends on a constant focus on strategy.

Visionary leadership: This brand of leadership is directed towards meeting long-term, lofty, significant goals. A visionary leader is motivated by a vision of the future. Visionary leaders often can effectively motivate others to work toward this vision. They create huge, but specific, achievable goals, and their leadership style can contain a balance of wisdom, practicality, and motivation or it can lack an appreciation of how difficult and risky it is to change a currently existing environment.

CATEGORY 15
HOLISTIC FOLLOWER

Fusion leadership: This brand of leadership has been popularized by Richard L. Daft and Robert H. Lengel in their book, *Fusion Leadership: Unlocking the Subtle Forces That Change People and Organizations.* Fusion leadership brings individuals together in order to accomplish a goal based on common vision and values.

Fusion leaders seek to engage the whole person: the bodies, minds, hearts, and souls of their followers. They support personal growth and creative thinking among followers in order to facilitate change. Fusion leadership depends on the belief that organizations function as living things. Part of the goal of fusion leadership is to fuse the organization and the individual followers and leaders of the organization, so that they grow and change together, in similar directions.

Generative leadership: This brand of leadership taught by Drexel Sprecher and others is a type of leadership that does not emphasize influencing other people. Instead, it aims to create an environment in which people continually deepen their understanding of reality, thereby becoming more capable of shaping their own futures. Generative leaders use their abilities to help their followers envision new futures, to articulate them, and, achieve them.

Transformational leadership: James MacGregor Burns is given credit for bringing the concept of transformational leadership to the center stage of leadership study and practice. Peter Northouse's book, *Leadership: Theory and Practice,* defines transformational leadership as a brand of leadership that makes people want to improve themselves and to be led. Successful transformational leaders are able to assess their followers' needs and show them they are valuable.

Four factors are included in transformational leadership: (1) Idealized influence—leaders who are trustworthy and are good role models; (2) Inspirational motivation—leaders who can motivate people to commit themselves to the ideals of an organization; (3) Intellectual stimulation—leaders encourage new ideas and critical thinking; and (4) Individual consideration—leaders coach their followers on how to use their strengths and reduce the liabilities of their weaknesses in a constructive way. Transformational leadership emphasizes the needs and strong roles of followers, as well as the reciprocal nature of the leadership/followership relationship.

CATEGORY 16
HOLISTIC LEADER FOCUS

Alpha leadership: This brand of leadership, which is distinct from the alpha male brand of leadership, is designed to maximize the effectiveness of leaders while helping them lead more balanced lives. According to Anne Deering, Robert Dilts, and Julian Russell, authors of *Alpha Leadership: Tools for Business Leaders Who Want More from Life,* alpha leadership contains three leadership areas: anticipate, align, and act.

Balanced leadership: This brand of leadership actually has several meanings. It refers to the appropriate balance of numerous personality traits to allow a leader to perform leadership tasks in an integrated manner. Balanced leaders realize that in order to be effective, they must carefully develop and cultivate their mental, emotional, and physical traits in the proper proportions for a given job. Balanced leadership can also refer to a leadership style that is, in actuality, a combination of several different types of leadership. In certain situations a leader may govern one way, whereas in others he or she may use a different method.

Continuous leadership: This brand of leadership builds on the definition of *leadership at every step.* The idea underlying leadership at every step is that leadership is a full-time activity and every action of a leader must be consistent. Continuous leadership expands on this concept and refers to people who are leaders at all times. Continuous leadership involves acting as a role model for one's followers and living what one teaches.

Enlightened leadership: This type of leadership, according to Ed Oakley and Doug Krug, authors of *Enlightened Leadership: Getting to the Heart of Change,* is represented by the efforts of leaders to make the most out of underutilized talent, expertise, and energy within an organization. Enlightened leadership plays a critical role in mobilizing these latent forces.

As Stephen Covey mentions, it works from the inside out. Enlightened leaders first become fully cognizant of their own strengths and weaknesses before evaluating others. Enlightened leaders view problems as opportunities for personal growth, both for the followers and for the leader. Enlightened leadership creates an environment of trust and helpfulness, which increases the morale of the followers.

Integral leadership: This brand of leadership has been popularized by Ken Wilber. It requires leaders to combine cognitive understanding and technical knowledge with several types of personal consciousness.

Total leadership: This brand of leadership focuses on team development, personal growth, and 360-degree feedback. Dr. Stephen Payne, leadership strategist and pioneer of the total leadership brand, claims that total leaders both achieve better business results and are more fulfilled in their personal lives. Total leadership is designed to integrate work, personal goals, family, and the community.

Wholehearted leadership: This brand of leadership, developed by Dusty Staub and Staub Leadership Consultants, uses the human heart as a model. Because the heart consists of four chambers, wholehearted leadership consists of four main quadrants: competency, integrity, passion, and intimacy. At the core of wholehearted leadership is a purpose, or goal, and in order to reach this goal, vision and courage are needed. Competency requires being able to understand and deal with the problem at hand and having the commitment to solve it. Integrity involves leading from a moral compass, and indicates that ethics play a vital role in wholehearted leadership.

Wholehearted leadership is rooted in strong interpersonal relationships that help to transfer the values of leaders to followers. Passion comes from the leaders' commitment to achieving certain goals and involves the creation of positive working environments. It also demonstrates the leader's commitment to service. Lastly, intimacy is what makes relationships last, and it allows leaders to show that they care about their followers and the community at large. The wholehearted leader's ability to lead successfully is also based on understanding and meeting the needs of their followers.

Appendix C

Defining a Future Leadership Research Agenda

Focusing on Teachers and their Impact on Student Performance and Student Outcomes

INTRODUCTION

We applaud those, including Educational Testing Service, The Education Commission for the States, Douglas Reeves, Joseph Murphy, McREL, McBassi & Company, and many, many others, who have ventured into conducting research on leadership for educators. While much of the focus has been on measuring leadership qualities and competencies of school administrators and their impact on student performance, more and more of the discussion is now focusing on measuring the leadership capabilities of teachers and measuring the impact of changes in the leadership capabilities of teachers on student outcomes.

The work of analyzing the impact of one variable on student achievement is very challenging. The existing research on teacher leadership has focused primarily on identifying the instructional processes and techniques that constitute superior practice and result in greater student achievement.

THE CURRENT STATE OF KNOWLEDGE

The empirical research we have found on measuring the leadership capabilities of teachers is very limited. While much has been written in a case study manner on leadership roles that teachers can, do, and should play that go beyond instruction processes and techniques, we urge funding for larger scale systematic research efforts to measure teachers on their knowledge, interest, and use of leadership competencies in the school workplace.

FUNDING FUTURE RESEARCH ON THE
IMPACT OF IMPROVED LEADERSHIP

Research is expensive, but new information technology, especially Web-based survey technology is bringing down the cost of this research. Research can now be created that focuses on "acts of leadership"—the behaviors and practices that teachers who seek to be leaders engage in that transcend and go beyond their role as instructional leaders. We have identified many acts of leadership which teachers can embark upon quickly.

We have recommended that teachers be trained in leadership, and research can be conducted as to how teachers evaluate this training and measure for themselves how this training impacts their ability to improve their schools, their students' outcomes, their levels of job satisfaction, and their expected and actual longevity in the teaching profession.

Knowing a little about school funding and knowing a little about how property values have recently plummeted, we know local school districts are not going to be able to fund significant research in this area. We also know that large-scale, truly useful research must be conducted at many schools at once, so there is little room for one school to conduct research that will be able to shape public policy and public opinion in the future.

However, that being said, we applaud schools, researchers, graduate students, and professional researchers working at one school of interest to begin to address some of the research design issues that will need to be addressed for a strong evolution of research methods to be developed and tested in this field.

USING THE LATEST RESEARCH AND
INFORMATION TECHNOLOGIES

We believe that this research agenda can be formulated in a community input fashion using Web 2.0 technologies, wikis, and blogs, and that many people would be willing to participate in this endeavor. The idea of an "open-source" generated set of research tools and methods has a strong potential in this field. Since Web 2.0 can achieve a scale quite rapidly, we urge the secretary of education to set aside funds and begin to financially support research on leadership for teachers.

We recommend that state education leaders share all of the information their agencies have and gain along the way so no one has to reinvent the wheel. We recommend that webinars and virtually developed conferences be set up to foster leadership development among teachers and foster excellent research in this field. We recommend that new journals, or journals currently in existence that are willing to "reset," begin publishing articles on a regular basis about how teachers can be better leaders and how we can document that they are in fact becoming better leaders.

POTENTIAL IMPACT OF FUTURE RESEARCH

Once we document that teachers are becoming better leaders and are pursuing more acts of leadership than they did before, then we can begin to document how the changes in leadership behavior are impacting student outcomes. There is already a well-developed concept called "benchmarking" that captures a phenomenon at a particular point in time in order to compare that activity or behavior at some point in the future.

Benchmarking leadership acts of teachers can be started right away with virtually no research budget and the results can be stored on a wiki or a Web site so others can emulate this beginning stage of research in this vitally important area.

Below we outline some of the research items that can be addressed in the very short term.

RESEARCH OBJECTIVES AND KEY QUESTIONS

Objective #1

Document the extent to which teachers are, in fact, viewed as leaders by themselves, their colleagues, administrators, and students

Key Questions

- What percentage of teachers view themselves as leaders?
- What percentage of school administrators (principals, superintendents) view teachers as leaders?
- What percentage of students view their teachers as leaders?

Objective #2

Identify the key behavioral differences between teachers who:

- Perceive themselves to be leaders and those who do not
- Are perceived by their peers to be leaders and those who are not perceived by their peers to be leaders

- Are perceived by their students to be leaders and those who are not perceived by their students to be leaders
- Are perceived by their administrators (principals, superintendent) to be leaders and those who are not perceived by their administrators to be leaders

Key Questions

- What are the key behavioral differences between teachers who view themselves as leaders and those who don't?
- What are the key behavioral differences between teachers who are widely acknowledged by their peers to be leaders and those who aren't?
- What are the key behavioral differences between teachers who are perceived by their students to be leaders and those who are not?
- What are the key behavioral differences between teachers who work in schools where their principal views them as leaders and those whose principals do not view them as leaders?

Objective #3

Determine the impact that teacher leadership has on student achievement and school learning environments.

Key Questions

- What are the differences in achievement of students whose teachers view themselves as leaders and those whose teachers do not view themselves as leaders?
- What are the differences in achievement of students in schools where a high percentage of teachers view themselves as leaders and students in schools where a low percentage of teachers do not view themselves as leaders?
- What are the key behavioral and achievement differentials between students who perceive their teacher as a leader and those who do not?

Objective #4

Determine which development opportunities appear to be especially promising for helping teachers to enhance their leadership skills

Key Questions

- What are the key behavioral differences in teachers who are perceived by their students to be leaders and those teachers who are not perceived by their students to be leaders?

- What are the differences in background and experience between teachers who view themselves as leaders and those who do not?
- Why do some teachers view themselves as leaders and others do not?
- What development experiences appear to be especially promising in helping teachers to become more effective leaders?

RESEARCH DESIGN

Unit of Analysis

Answering these questions will require that a variety of different "units of analysis" be used. Many of the questions will be addressed by using an individual—a teacher, a student, a school administrator—as the unit of analysis. Other questions will best be addressed by using classrooms as the unit of analysis, while still others will be addressed using schools as the unit of analysis.

Methodology

Carefully constructed *surveys* will be a critical research tool for answering many of the questions outlined above. In particular, those questions that focus on the perception of teachers as leaders—by themselves, their peers, their students, and administrators—will best be answered through surveys.

Detailed *observation* of teachers—both inside and outside of their classrooms—will be the best methodology for answering questions about the behavioral differences of teachers who are perceived as leaders (by themselves, their peers, their students, and administrators) and those who are not.

Quantitative analysis that relies on *"quasi-experimental design"* estimation techniques (that control for the effects of confounding variables) will be useful for analyzing the impact of various teacher leadership practices on student achievement, as well as schools' learning environments. In many cases the data collected through surveys (as noted above) will be combined with student, classroom, and school-level outcomes for the purpose of linking measures of teacher leadership to the outcomes of interest.

Randomized experimentation, which is often considered to be the gold standard of research design, will have limited (if any) relevance for answering the questions outlined above. The analysis of leadership is simply not a topic that lends itself to being analyzed through experiments.

Action research will be useful for answering questions about the types of leadership interventions that are most effective in enhancing teachers' leadership skills.

FUNDING

Many of the research questions outlined above can only be answered with large sample sizes (of teachers and schools). Hence, it will be beyond the capabilities—both because of their limited size and budgets—of many school districts to be able to undertake this research effectively. Consequently, much of this research will require funding from foundations, state agencies, and/or the federal government to be able to achieve the necessary scale.

Those questions that can best be answered through action research can be done within schools and/or school districts. But even this research would benefit greatly from having a significant number of teachers involved—all using a consistent research design—across multiple schools and districts. As a result, external funding and research design will be essential for maximizing learning.

The funds of foundations can likely be tapped for some of this research. Government funds at the federal level could be available as well. We urge teachers not to rely exclusively on the Secretary of Education or your school administrators or your school district or State administrators to be the sole voices in support of this research. We urge teachers to take action to let it be known that this research is important to them and to their future visions for their schools and their profession.

CONCLUSION

Research can be performed at the school level, at the school district level, at the state level, and the national level. It can be quantitative and it can be qualitative. We urge teachers to begin to demand that schools conduct research on many aspects of leadership as it relates to teachers. It will take a decade to build a robust body of data and information on the level of leadership knowledge, skills, and abilities that teachers possess in the United States.

Once we understand the level of leadership skills our teachers have, we can design better training and leadership development programs to fill the gaps. In addition, we can begin to assess how significantly improving leadership skills of teachers positively impacts student outcomes, teacher satisfaction and longevity, overall school performance, funding levels for schools, and many other factors that are critical to schools in our nations.

The research we propose can be conducted for all teachers, coaches, librarians, special needs teachers, staff, administrators, and any segment of the school population. We believe additional research should be performed around student evaluations. This area of research has proven very valuable at the university level, and we find no reason to believe it could not be beneficial for many grades in the PreK–12 educational arena.

Leadership on research must come from the federal government as well. The Secretary of Education has a special responsibility to fund research on the impact of improving leadership skills of teachers on how schools and students perform. We urge teachers' unions and all associations that promote PreK–12 education in the United States to join us in our efforts to have the federal government allocate substantial funding for research in the area of leadership development for educators.

Bibliography

Ackerman, R. H., & Mackenzie, S. V. (2007). *Uncovering Teacher Leadership: Essays and Voices from the Field.* Thousand Oaks, CA: Corwin Press.

Austin Independent School District. (n.d.) *Teacher Leadership Development Program.* Retrieved March 5, 2009, from http://www.austinisd.org/teachers/teacher_leadership/

Blase, J., & Blase, J. (2001). *Empowering Teachers: What Successful Principals Do* (2nd ed.). Thousand Oaks, CA: Corwin Press.

Boyatizis, R. E., & McKee, A. (2005). *Resonant Leadership: Renewing Yourself and Connecting With Others Through Mindfulness, Hope, and Compassion.* Boston: Harvard Business School Press.

Brevard Public Schools. (2005, May 24). *Appointment of Dori A. Bisbey to the position of staff development specialist, 10-month contract.* School Board of Brevard County (Board Agenda Item F-5). Retrieved March 5, 2009, from http://www.brevard.k12.fl.us/School_Board/meet_min_agen/PDF%20May%2024%202005/F-5.pdf

Childs-Bowen, D., Moller, G., & Scrivner, J. (2000, May). Principals: Leaders of leaders. *NASSP Bulletin, 84*(616), 27–34.

Crown Consortium. (2006). *Leadership Development for Teachers (LDT).* Retrieved March 5, 2009, from http://wsm.ezsitedesigner.com/pdf/LEADERSHIP%20DEVELOPMENT%20 FOR%20TEACHERS.pdf

Crowther, F., Kaagan, S.S., Ferguson, M., & Hann, L. (2009). *Developing Teacher Leaders: How Teacher Leadership Enhances School Success* (2nd ed.). Thousand Oaks, CA: Corwin Press.

Danielson, C. (2006). *Teacher Leadership That Strengthens Professional Practice.* Alexandria, VA: Association for Supervision and Curriculum Development.

Donaldson, G. A. (2001). *Cultivating Leadership in Schools: Connecting People, Purpose, and Practice.* New York: Teachers College Press.

Durrant, J., & Holden, G. (2005). *Teachers Leading Change: Doing Research for School Improvement (Leading Teachers, Leading Schools Series)*. London: Paul Chapman.

Feiler, R., Heritage, M., & Gallimore, R. (2000, April). *Teachers Leading Teachers. Educational Leadership, 57*(7), 66-69.

Fink, D. (2005). *Leadership for Mortals: Developing and Sustaining Leaders of Learning (Leading Teachers, Leading Schools Series)*. London: Paul Chapman.

Fullan, M. (1999). *Change Forces: The Sequel*. Philadelphia: Falmer Press.

Fullan, M. (2004). *Leading in a Culture of Change: Personal Action Guide and Workbook*. San Francisco: Jossey-Bass.

Fullan, M. (2004). *The Moral Imperative of School Leadership*. Thousand Oaks, CA: Corwin Press.

Fullan, M. (2005). *Leadership and Sustainability: System Thinkers in Action*. Thousand Oaks, CA: Corwin Press.

Green, R. L. (2009). *Practicing the Art of Leadership: A Problem-Based Approach to Implementing the ISLLC Standards*. Boston: Pearson Allyn & Bacon.

Harris, A., & Lambert, L. (2003). *Building Leadership Capacity for School Improvement*. Berkshire: Open University Press.

Harris, A., & Mujis, D. (2005). *Improving Schools Through Teacher Leadership*. Berkshire: Open University Press.

Hay Group Education (2004, July). *The Five Pillars of Distributed Leadership in Schools: An Investigation in to the Advantages and Disadvantages, Causes and Constraints of a More Distributed Form of Leadership in Schools*. National College for School Leadership.

Katzenmeyer, M., & Moller, G. (1996). *Every Teacher as a Leader: Realizing the Potential of Teacher Leadership*. San Francisco: Jossey-Bass.

Katzenmeyer, M., & Moller, G. (2001). *Awakening The Sleeping Giant: Leadership Development for Teachers*. Thousand Oaks, CA: Corwin Press. (ERIC Document Reproduction Service No. ED399680)

Kotter, J. P. (1996). *Leading Change*. Boston: Harvard Business School Press.

Kouzes, J. M., & Posner, B. Z. (2003). *Credibility: How Leaders Gain It and Lose It; Why People Demand It*. San Francisco: Jossey-Bass.

Kouzes, J. M., & Posner, B. Z. (2003). *The Leadership Challenge* (rev. ed.). San Francisco: Jossey-Bass.

Marzano, R. J., Waters, T., & McNulty, B. A. (2005). *School Leadership That Works: From Research to Results*. Alexandria, VA: Association for Supervision and Curriculum Development.

Merideth, E. M. (2006). *Leadership Strategies for Teachers*. Thousand Oaks, CA: Corwin Press.

Murphy, J. (2002). *The Educational Leadership Challenge: Redefining Leadership for the 21st Century*. Chicago: University of Chicago Press.

Murphy, J. F. (2005). *Connecting teacher leadership and school improvement*. Thousand Oaks, CA: Corwin Press.

Quinn, C., Haggard, C., & Ford, B. (2006, February). *Preparing New Teachers for Leadership Roles: A Model in Four Phases. School Leadership and Management,* 26(1), 55–64.

Reeves, D. B. (2002). *The Daily Disciplines of Leadership: How to Improve Student Achievement, Staff motivation, and Personal Organization.* San Francisco: Jossey-Bass.

Reeves, D. B. (2004). *Accountability for Learning: How Teachers and School Leaders Can Take Charge.* Alexandria, VA: Association for Supervision and Curriculum Development.

Reeves, D. B. (2006). *The Learning Leader: How to Focus School Improvement for Better Results.* Alexandria, VA: Association for Supervision and Curriculum Development.

Rubenstein, Herb (2008). *Leadership for Lawyers.* Chicago: American Bar Association.

Savage, Anika and Sales, Michael. *Anticipatory Leadership. Strategy and Leadership,* Volume 38, No 6, 2008, pp. 28–35, United Kingdom: Emerald Group Publishing.

Sergiovanni, T. J. (1989). *Value-Added Leadership: How to Get Extraordinary Performance in Schools.* San Diego: Harcourt, Brace, & Jovanovich.

Sergiovanni, T. J. (2001). *The Lifeworld of Leadership.* San Francisco: Jossey-Bass.

Sparks, D. (2005). *Leading for Results: Transforming Teaching, Learning, and Relationships in Schools.* Thousand Oaks, CA: Corwin Press.

Stone, R., & Cuper, P. H. (2006). *Best Practices for Teacher Leadership: What Award-Winning Teachers Do for Their Professional Learning Communities.* Thousand Oaks, CA: Corwin Press.

Tapscott, D., & Williams, A. D. (2006). *Wikinomics: How Mass Collaboration Changes Everything.* New York: Portfolio.

University of West Georgia College of Education. (2006, February 15). *Teacher as Leader.* Department of early childhood education and reading (Lesson Plan ECED 8272). Retrieved March 5, 2009, from http://coe.westga.edu/syllabi/eced/ECED8272.pdf

Wilmore, E. L. (2007). *Teacher Leadership: Improving Teaching and Learning From Inside the Classroom.* Thousand Oaks, CA: Corwin Press.

About the Authors

Herb Rubenstein is a Phi Beta Kappa graduate of Washington and Lee University where he was elected to Omicron Delta Kappa, the national collegiate leadership society, and served as the student representative to the curriculum committee and curses and degrees committee of the University. Upon graduation from college, he received a Rotary Foundation Scholarship to do graduate study in sociology at the University of Bristol in England. He then became Lyndon Johnson Scholar and received his M.P.A. from the Lyndon B. Johnson School of Public Affairs of the University of Texas at Austin. After working at the National Academy of Sciences and the American Institutes for Research, he joined the United States Department of Health and Human Services, developing education, training, and employment programs for people receive public assistance. Thereafter, he received his law degree from Georgetown University and served as a partner in his Washington, D.C.-based law firm for over twenty years. He has served as a volunteer development director for public schools in Maryland and currently is assisting in Colorado with the development of a large-scale volunteer program that will serve as a national pilot program for public school districts throughout the country. He is the co-author of *Breakthrough, Inc.: High Growth Strategies for Entrepreneurial Organizations* (Financial Times/Prentice Hall, 1999), the author of *Leadership for Lawyers* (American Bar Association, 2nd ed., 2008), plus over a hundred published articles on leadership and organizational effectiveness. He is the president of the Sustainable Business Group, a consulting firm to educational institutions, businesses, nonprofit organizations, and government agencies. He directs the firm's Sustainable Leadership Academy (www.sbizgroup.com).

Mike Miles holds degrees from the United States Military Academy at West Point, the University of California at Berkeley, and Columbia University. He has served the public interest as a soldier, statesman, and educator. A former officer in the Army Ranger Battalion, Miles's military experience includes leading counterterrorism training operations. Miles later served in the U.S. State Department as a Soviet analyst and member of the Bureau of Intelligence and Research. He then served as a diplomat to Poland and Russia at the end of the Cold War, finishing his State Department work as the special assistant to the ambassador to Russia. He currently serves as the superintendent of schools in the Harrison School District in Colorado Springs. Under his leadership, Harrison has made significant achievement gains and is recognized as a "turnaround district." Mike Miles has developed leadership rubrics, leadership curricula, and has delivered leadership development seminars to teachers and employees at every level in the school districts where he has served.

Laurie Bassi holds a Ph.D. in economics from Princeton, a master's degree from the Industrial and Labor Relations School of Cornell University, and a B.S. in mathematics from Illinois State University. Laurie Bassi is an authority on human capital management—the processes and practices that align the management and development of employees with and organization's results. She has overseen the development of the McBassi People Index™, an intensively-researched tool for pinpointing and improving the human capital drivers of an organization's results (www.mcbassi.com). Dr. Bassi has successfully conducted surveys of teachers and analyzed data from these surveys in order to improve student performance and teacher performance in public schools. Prior to founding McBassi & Company, Laurie served as the director of research for ASTD, director of two U.S. government commissions, and co-chair of the National Academy of Sciences' Board on Testing and Assessment. The early years of Laurie's career were spent as a tenured professor of economics at Georgetown University. Dr. Bassi has authored over eighty published papers and books and has served on committees of the National Academy of Sciences dealing with PreK–12 education in the United States.